AMC Field Guide to Trail Building and Maintenance

by Robert D. Proudman
AMC Trail Supervisor

Photographs by George Bellerose

Illustrations by Marc Lacroix,
Jean Farquhar and Janis Merkle

CONTENTS

PUBLISHER'S PREFACE

THE TRAIL — IT'S SOMETHING hikers, campers, cross-country skiers and other users may not think much about, may perhaps even take for granted. That is, until it is lost through improper marking, or until it becomes a mosquito-infested swamp through poor drainage. Then, and perhaps only then, do we realize that the trail is the essential medium without which our sport would be impossible.

A change seems to be in the wind, though. The hiker and his trails are becoming important considerations in outdoor recreation and backcountry management. Witness the heavy interest in low-impact hiking and camping techniques, the spate of pamphlets and articles on shelter and trail development, and cover stories recently in *Newsweek* and *U.S. News and World Report* on outdoor recreation.

A recent Nielsen poll listed camping as the fourth-largest participant sport in America, with 58.1 million people involved. Camping is also among the ten fastest growing participant sports, registering a 7% growth rate between 1973 and 1976. Other outdoor sports that impact on trails, although less directly than camping, are also among the 25 largest participant sports: bicycling, hunting, fishing, skiing, snowmobiling and motorcycling.

We are, in short, becoming an outdoor-oriented nation, and we seem to be finding the leisure time to pursue our outdoor interests. As the population grows, and the population of trail users grows even faster, pressure on limited, and perhaps shrinking, facilities grows commensurately.

The Appalachian Mountain Club has been interested in trails longer than most organizations, including the federal government. The Club's trail crew program is over half a century old. Its budget has increased tenfold since the sixties.

With the increased interest in trails nationally, AMC's long years of experience and the many dollars spent are suddenly starting to be recognized, not only in the Club's traditional White Mountain domain, but in other areas around the country, and even internationally.

This book is the distillation of that expertise. By Robert D. Proudman, AMC's trail supervisor, it covers all the skills and equipment needed to plan, build and maintain trails. Obviously, the book is intended for anyone, anywhere in the world, who is responsible for such activities — government agencies, outing clubs, hiking groups, ski touring centers and nonprofit organizations involved in outdoor recreation and backcountry management. Less obviously, it is also for every recreational user. Each of us who spends time on the trail should understand how fragile it is, and how much work goes into its care and feeding. Only then will we respect it properly. And perhaps only then will we be willing to work to save that endangered species — the trail.

Arlyn S. Powell, Jr.
Director of Publications
Appalachian Monutain Club

CREDITS AND ACKNOWLEDGMENTS

THIS BOOK HAS TRULY BEEN A COOPERATIVE effort by volunteers, members and staff of the Appalachian Mountain Club (AMC), as well as by outside groups. Countless individuals and organizations have made contributions.

The current AMC trail crew deserves the credit for developing or adapting from outside sources the techniques described here. Past trailmasters, crew leaders and members have also contributed in a dynamic way to the evolution of the concepts now being used in trail design, building and maintenance.

This book could not have been done without the leadership, encouragement and dynamic example set by J. Joseph May, AMC trails supervisor from 1961 to 1971. Joe made possible a climate where crew members were encouraged to think and to employ new ideas and concepts to manage the problems that had to be faced on trails.

This, in turn, could not have taken place without the trust and good will of the Appalachian Mountain Club. The AMC executive staff, Trail Committee and Executive Council have permitted experimentation and have prodded for positive results through investment of Club funds in the trails program. Despite competing needs in other Club areas, as well as a recessionary and inflationary economy, money has always been confidently allocated to the growing needs that have become evident in our trail system.

Reuben Rajala, AMC trails coordinator, has donated many hours of review for all sections of this book. He also wrote parts of the first draft of the trail reconstruction and tools sections. Sally Surgenor, AMC research assistant, wrote the first draft of the section on soils. Ed Spencer, AMC research director, wrote the section on vegetation, as well as parts of the reconstruction chapter.

Artists Marc Lacroix and Jean Farquhar sketched several drafts of each drawing and completed a demanding agenda of art work. George Bellerose provided the fine photographs that illustrate the book.

Members of the trail crew who helped write and review sections include Steve Rice, Jon Vara, Bruce Davis, Jon Coe and Bill Birchard. Many unnamed crew members laid down their hand tools and took pen in hand to convey their working techniques.

Much of the information on signs has been provided by our sign maker for many years, the late Clyde Smith. Clyde's craftsmanship is visible in many signs up and down the Appalachian Trail.

The Forest Service, U. S. Department of Agriculture (USDA), helped directly through staff assistance, particularly — from Ray Leonard at the USDA Northeast Forest Station — as well as indirectly through their publications and bulletins. Staff members of the White Mountain National Forest have contributed in their steward's

TRAIL BUILDING AND MAINTENANCE

role as managers of the National Forest that contains most of AMC's trail system.

The Appalachian Trail Conference, through its volunteers, staff and publications, has contributed, as has the Society for the Protection of New Hampshire Forests, whose help made possible the section on private land.

The AMC Publications Department, under the leadership of W. Kent Olson, provided professional guidance, especially in final drafts and production. The AMC Department of Financial Resources, under the direction of Sam Rogers, wrote proposals that eventually led to funding of the manuscript.

The Howard and Bush Foundation in Hartford, Connecticut, showed exemplary confidence and foresight in funding an unfinished manuscript.

Tom Deans, AMC Executive Director, deserves credit for his trust, guidance and enforcement of unpleasant but nonetheless essential deadlines.

And finally, and in a practical sense most importantly, much credit goes to Kim Smith, my secretary, and the office staff at Pinkham Notch Camp for their prompt and cheerful typing, copying and editing of countless drafts of this book.

Robert D. Proudman
Pinkham Notch Camp, New Hampshire
Spring, 1977

INTRODUCTION

THE APPALACHIAN MOUNTAIN CLUB has for many years been a moving force behind hiking programs in the northeastern United States. Club officers and members have actively mapped, designed and built many of the hiking trails that exist in this area today, providing access into the area's most beautiful mountain back-country.

In 1920 Club officers instituted a professional trail crew, the first of its kind in the country. This crew was based in the White Mountains of New Hampshire, where it developed and maintained trails primarily for Club members and programs. Today the crew consists of thirty seasonal employees and two full-time staff members who are responsible for approximately 375 miles of trails and 17 shelters and campsites in the White Mountain region.

Beginning in the early 1960's increased public use of AMC facilities became apparent. Tabulations made at more popular campsites since 1970 have shown an aver-

1924 Trail Crew

1976 Trail Crew

age increase in the use of White Mountain trails of 10-15% per year. The AMC trail crew has grown to meet the greater needs that have been developing with this increasing public use. The Club's trails budget in 1965 was $10,000; in 1975 it was $100,000.

The programs financed by this money have grown in complexity as well as size. The historical function of the crew has been simply to clear brush and keep trails marked. There are stories of how the crew visited roadside campgrounds to solicit hikers to tramp down the trails and so to help keep them open. The situation today is considerably different. Unprecedented numbers of visitors have taxed the physical ability of soils and plantlife to remain healthy and stable under the pressure of great volumes of traffic. Aggravated erosion on slopes is rampant on many mountain trails. Sanitation problems and litter disposal have degraded the areas used for overnight camping.

The AMC trail crew has developed programs to meet these new demands. This book is an effort to distill and describe the best of the techniques that have been developed. These techniques are applicable to some degree to all foot trails, so they can be employed and further adapted to solve similar trail problems in other popular mountain areas. All techniques described have been developed through the trial and error of practical application in the field.

Coupled with the need to improve environmental trail management at popular facilities in our mountain parks and forests is a growing need to implement trail programs to build new trails and to protect existing trails on the local, town and county levels. Second home development and competing trail use from off-road vehicles have forced some trails to close. Trail development on privately-owned local property provides recreational opportunities nearer to home. Town, county and state parks are more available if access is eased using trail development.

Residents can then gain local recreational opportunities normally reserved for vacation times and for places removed from their day-to-day community environment.

The trails program of the Appalachian Mountain Club exemplifies the advantages of private, charitable and non-profit development of public recreational facilities and programs. The freedom to work on dynamic new projects, the enthusiasm generated by such work and the resulting low cost are extremely beneficial when viewed as complementary components to traditional state and federal trail programs.

It is our hope that in publishing this book we can stimulate similar private trail groups, as well as outing clubs, community groups and interested individuals, to take a more active part in trail development, maintenance and protection before use damages sensitive high country, and before development pressures on the land from private enterprise foreclose new trail opportunities that are America's birthright. There is common cause to unify and develop a national program to protect the rights of our citizens to travel on foot through natural settings, unfettered in the pursuit of this most fundamental recreational activity.

1

DESIGNING TRAILS

*The job of recreational engineering is not one of build-
ing trails into lovely country, but of building receptivity
into the yet unloving human mind.*

Aldo Leopold

TRAILS DESIGNED so that they provide satisfying recreational access into natural areas are the primary goal
of the techniques in this book. Reviewing of some basic
guidelines for locating and maintaining trails will ensure that the resulting facilities can provide opportunities for meeting the recreational needs of hikers.

The trail should "fit" by maintaining continuity and
regularity in the way it traverses land. Sudden changes
in direction or too much meandering should be avoided.
Likewise, long, straight sections should be used temper-
ately; they lack interest for hikers.

There should be regularity in clearing and marking
throughout the trail's length. For example, changing the
way a trail is marked midway along its length will cause
hikers confusion. This also applies to trails that are climbing a slope. Hikers using such trails should not have to
lose significant elevation unnecessarily because of poor

design. The trail should be consistent in climbing into the high country if this is its function.

Cultural and historic features such as old dam and mill sites, cellar holes and old village sites can add historical and educational dimensions to a trail design. Research into an area's cultural features should be done in order to optimize the value of a trail's location. Interpretive information in guidebooks and on signs can make this information available to walkers.

In some cases the reputation of a feature, be it a natural one such as a mountain summit or a manmade one such as a village site or an old mine, may be great enough to attract use even though trail access does not exist. In these cases it may be advisable to install a trail in order to contain traffic on a well-planned route. Several trailless summits in the Adirondacks of New York have been damaged because hikers have visited these summits using "bootleg" trails. An excessive number of unplanned trails approach these summits like the spokes of a wheel approaching the hub. If a well-designed trail provides access, damage from trampling to these sensitive alpine summits can be reduced.

One of the greatest highlights a trail can offer is the scenic vista. The traveler should have the feeling that, for the most part, the land mass is below him at such vistas.

All trails have terminuses, which are respectively the *trailhead* or start of the trail (usually located at roadside) and the *destination*, be it a mountain summit, waterfall, mill site or similar feature. Destinations in a system of trails will, for any single trail, include other trails and campsites.

The choice of route, in addition to connecting these terminuses and maintaining regular marking standards, slope and direction, should incorporate beautiful and dramatic natural features. Diverse biological, climatic

and topographical characteristics should be condensed into short sections of trail wherever possible. Outlooks, rock outcrops, stream sides and similar features of the landscape please the traveler and therefore should be integrated into the trail location. High-quality trail design is primarily a balance between beauty and function. Natural features and scenery exist ideally in creative combination with the continuity, efficiency and durability of a proposed route.

Anatomy of a Trail

A trail is made up of components, the sum of which make up the total view of the trail environment seen by the hiker. The following is a description of these components — what they are and how they complement each other in the design of a trail. Defining these terms now will assist in understanding subsequent chapters.

The *trail treadway* or *trail tread* is the surface upon which the hiker makes direct contact with the soil. It is the location for virtually all improvements that ease

hiker passage by hardening and stabilizing soils from shifting, eroding or becoming muddy. Popular trails will damage soils on slopes and in wet terrain; therefore, good maintenance of the treadway occasionally requires reconstruction and rehabilitation of the original soil profile. The treadway is the most important component of any foot trail.

The trail *right-of-way* is the area around the treadway that is cleared for passage of the hiker. It is usually eight to twelve feet wide, depending on vegetation density. The term "right-of-way" also refers to legal right of passage, such as would be the case with a protected trail on private land.

The *trail corridor*[1] includes the treadway, right-of-way and all the lands that make up the environment of the trail as viewed by the hiker. The Forest Service calls it the "zone of travel influence." This terminology shows

---

[1]This material has been developed with reference to *Guidelines for the Appalachian Trail*, U.S. Department of the Interior, 1971.

that the corridor includes all those lands having an influence on the hiker's perception of the trail environment.

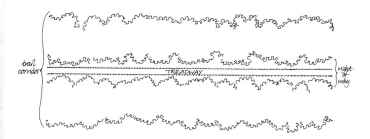

In particularly important trail systems, such as the Appalachian National Scenic Trail, this corridor takes on added importance. Legislation passed by the U.S. Congress requires that the corridor of the Appalachian Trail be protected from adverse developments that would be detrimental to its natural quality. However, acquisition of lands for control of timber harvesting and development activities is an expensive and difficult proposition. Therefore, definition of the corridor's width takes on critical importance. In some situations state and federal plans have defined the Appalachian Trail corridor as being two hundred feet wide, even though in open forests, on lake shores and above treeline this obviously does not include all the lands that influence the hiker. Managers of the Appalachian Trail are presently trying to define this corridor more accurately, in order to effectively protect the quality of the experience of walking along it.

The *buffer* or *protection zone* is the land area on each side of the trail treadway. The buffer zones, along with the treadway and the right-of-way, make up the total trail corridor. Buffer zones are the areas that insulate the hiker from activities detrimental to the hiking experience, such as second home development, mining or logging.

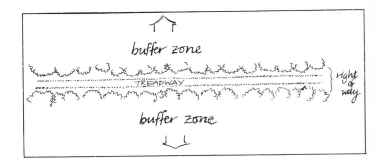

Buffers can also be used to protect particularly fragile areas from damage due to hikers. Trail layout around sensitive plantlife, lake shores and springs should include buffers to protect these fragile areas from trampling.

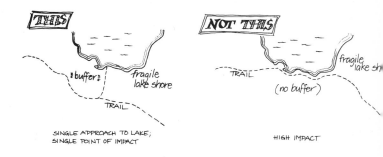

SINGLE APPROACH TO LAKE;
SINGLE POINT OF IMPACT

HIGH IMPACT

Formats for Trail System Design

There are three major formats that can be used in backcountry trail design.

The *loop* is a popular format for day-use trails because it enables easy access and parking. Hikers do not have to return on the same trail; therefore, interest and satisfaction in hiking a loop can be kept at a high level. Loops, especially if doubled into figure eights, can also be an efficient format for trail development in areas that are limited in size.

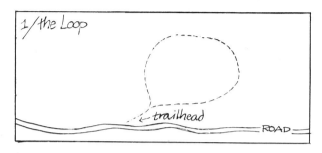

The *horseshoe* can be a valuable trail format, especially in areas where public transportation is available. It can also be used as an appropriate alternative to auto travel on roads where distances between treminuses are not too great. Ski touring trail development in the Mt. Washington Valley of New Hampshire has trailheads at inns and restaurants in the valley connected by trails in the horseshoe format.

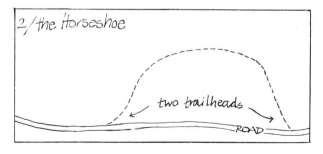

The *line* is the simplest and most common format for trails. It connects two points; e.g., the roadside trailhead and the destination, which may be a summit, waterfall or similar feature. A good example of trails in the line format are firewarden's trails to lookout towers on mountain summits. Long-distance trails such as the Appalachian Trail and Pacific Crest Trail are premiere examples of trails in the line format. These "trunk line" trails on public lands with high scenic value are augumented with side trails, alternate routes and connectors to form trail systems.

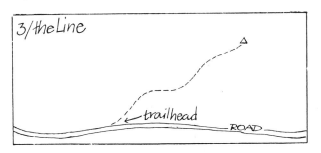

A *trail system* should use these different formats to satisfy a diversity of recreational needs. Careful design will provide trails for different users with different expectations. Multi-day backpackers as well as less adventurous walkers can be served by a well-designed trail system.

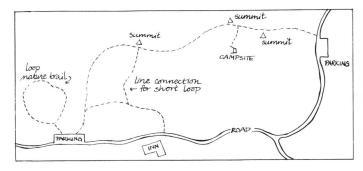

Trail Access

The type and volume of public access to a proposed trail is a powerful factor that needs to be studied carefully in its design. If a trailhead is proposed on a major recreational highway then we may accurately forecast that visitor use will be high; and therefore, for safety and to protect the resources of the proposed trail corridor, the standards of the trail must be correspondingly higher. This requirement for high standards means that planning must be more comprehensive and that the investment in design and construction must be substantial if the trail is to be safe, enjoyable and environmentally stable. The reverse is also true: if access is from an infrequently used rural road, then the standard of the proposed trail can be reduced and the cost and effort in planning, design and construction can be correspondingly lower.

The existence and size of parking facilities are important considerations in trail design. If the designer wants a reduced volume of use, then parking should be nonexistent or limited. If parking is plentiful, use will tend to increase, increasing the maintenance needs of the trail.

For reasons of safety, the location of parking facilities on highways must be carefully planned. Efforts at design and maintenance of parking facilities should be coordinated with the appropriate representatives of the State Highway Department or Department of Transportation. Their specifications for the location of a parking facility on a highway should, in a large part, determine the location of the trailhead.

Parking facilities should also be coordinated with other recreational uses. If a picnic area already exists, then placing the trailhead in this locale will obviously preclude the need for a new parking lot. If a snowmobile trail has parking available, then a summer hiking trail placed in the same vicinity will reduce the cost of building additional facilities.

Management of trailhead parking may additionally require that there be litter-collection facilities, signs and informational notices. These needs should be planned into a trail design so that no problems exist after installation.

A recreational trail should buffer the trail participant from man-made features such as roads, railroad tracks, logging operations and second home development. In cases where the trail must cross a road, railroad, logging operation or similar feature, the designer should place the trail so as to minimize the hiker's exposure to these debilitating characteristics. These areas should be crossed in the shortest practical manner, usually at right angles. Long lines of sight should be avoided.

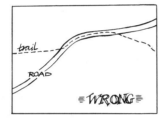 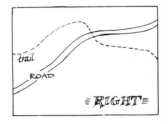

In addition to minimizing the negative experiential impact of road and railroad crossings, right angle crossings are also safer.

All of these general concepts should be refined to suit specific needs for the planning and design or maintenance of any particular trail. Any trail project, in order to be efficiently executed with high-quality results, should be thought through with proper consideration for the primary objective of meeting the recreational needs of hikers.

2

ENVIRONMENTAL CONSIDERATIONS
IN TRAIL DESIGN

A trail in the initial stages of erosion. (facing page)

Soil Characteristics

ENVIRONMENTAL DESIGN OF TRAILS requires that the designer pay close attention to the soil characteristics of the area in question. This chapter will give the reader a broad overview of soils and their characteristics, especially when subject to trampling from hiking.

Soil is a mixture of organic matter, water, mineral matter and air that comprises the root zone of living plants. Soil covers most of the surface of the earth and varies in thickness from inches to hundreds of feet. This covering of soil is like a mosaic, with different soil types and characteristics distinguishable from place to place. Each soil is composed of one or more *layers* or *horizons* that, when looked at as a unit, can be called the *soil profile.*

There are several ways in which soil fails to support hiking use:

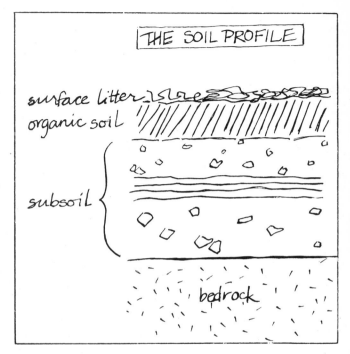

THE SOIL PROFILE

surface litter
organic soil

subsoil {

bedrock

Compaction — Hiking causes plants to bend, break and eventually to die. After this mortality, the surface horizons of soil compact into a cement-like hardness. This compacted surface loses its pore space and, therefore, its ability to absorb surface water. If this water is not absorbed into the compacted soil it will puddle on the trail or, if on a slope, will start to flow downhill causing erosion. Research has shown that a stream of water will flow up to 15 times farther on compacted soil than on soil in its naturally porous condition.[2]

---

[2]Winklaar, Paul, *Forest Road Location on Northern New Hampshire Soils*, Cooperative Extension Service, University of New Hampshire, Durham, August, 1971, p. 7.

Surface Erosion — Erosion is a natural process in which soils are worn away by the action of wind, water, glaciers and other natural phenomena. On trails this natural process is aggravated by soil compaction and the almost constant churning agitation of hiking traffic. Water flowing over the compacted soil surface detaches the smaller, lighter soil particles and carries them downhill. The greater the velocity of flowing water, the greater the mass of soil that can be carried. Velocity is increased as slope steepens. Increased volume of water run-off also increases velocity. At high elevations, greater amounts of water accumulate than in neighboring valleys. Ecological studies carried out in Vermont for six years have shown that greater amounts of rainfall occur at a 3600 foot elevation than at 1800 feet.

In addition to direct precipitation, the needles of spruce and fir trees, which dominate the landscape at high elevations, "comb" water from clouds.

These large volumes of water made more damaging by steep slopes and by foot traffic, create a particularly serious erosion hazard on trails in mountain areas. This erosion can quickly destroy a trail treadway. Research done in the Adirondacks indicates a soil loss of one inch per year on hiking trails.[3]

A treadway in the early stages of being eroded is easy to spot. Loose stones and gravel are left after the smaller, stabilizing sand and silt particles have been removed by water. These stones make for poor footing, which in turn causes the hiker to walk on the edge of the trail, thereby killing plants, compacting the soil and generally initiating a vicious circle of plant mortality, compaction and erosion that will eventually change a trail into a boulder-strewn gully.

---

[3]Ketchledge, E. H., and Leonard, R. E., "The Impact of Man on the Adirondack High Country," *The New York Conservationist*, October-November, 1970, pp. 14-18.

FROM THIS........   TO THIS

Erosion, in addition to causing uncertain footing and unsightly gulleys, can cause resource damage beyond the trail's treadway. After sediment-loaded water slows down, soil particles are deposited on the forest floor, suffocating smaller plantlife — and in serious situations even suffocating trees by covering up the lower trunks. If these sediments find their way into streams and ponds they can kill fish life and, by adding soil nutrients to water, accelerate the eutrophication of waterways. Soil loss around the base of trees can expose roots to disease and weaken their anchoring function, allowing trees to blow down much more easily.

Because of the possibilities for resource degradation, trail design, installation and maintenance in mountainous backcountry must employ a careful evaluation of soil characteristics in order to be successful. Wherever possible, trails should be located on soils that are capable of withstanding the amount of use anticipated without eroding or becoming wet and muddy.

This ability of soil to withstand traffic of a given intensity depends on several factors. In some cases a single factor can be limiting, so that soil will degrade swiftly despite other more enduring qualities it may possess. In other cases a combination of factors are important to consider in determining the best location for the trail. These factors are soil wetness, texture, structure and depth.

Soil Wetness — Soil wetness may be caused by poor drainage. *Ground water* moving through the landscape may saturate the surface of soils, especially during periods of heavy rainfall and the spring thaw. The level of ground water is called the *water table*. It fluctuates with the wetness of the season. The seasonally high water table is the highest level of ground water during the wettest month of the year. This seasonally high water table in shallow or poorly drained soils will cause surface springs and seeps which can cause problems on a compacted treadway. In very poorly drained soils, such as in bogs or depressions near lakes and streams, water moves so slowly that the soil surface may be wet for much of the year. Trails in such areas should be avoided.

Soil Wetness Indicators — There are several indicators that can be used to evaluate soil wetness in the field. The most obvious and simple evaluation is visiting the site during periods of high water run-off — after long periods of rainfall or during the spring snow melt. If much surface water is evident in many rivulets, then the site is limited in its appropriateness for trail location. Dig a shallow hole along the proposed trail site; if it fills with water or if water placed within it does not percolate down and out of the hole, then there is either a high water table or drainage is inhibited. In both cases trail use will degrade the environment.

The color of subsurface soils can be a practical clue to drainage conditions. Most soils contain some iron compounds which, if alternately exposed to air and water, oxidize to take on a reddish-brown color. Soils with these colors present can therefore indicate free movement of air and water as conditions of wetness change. It is likely that such soils are well drained and therefore appropriate for trail use if other conditions are not limiting.

An additional indication of good drainage is the uniformity of the soil's coloring. Uniform coloring can indicate free air and water movement through the soil. Correspondingly, "mottles" of red or yellow imposed on a uniform background indicate short periods of poor drainage, perhaps in the spring. Mottling or layering of gray or bluish-gray soil indicates longer or perennially poor drainage. In areas where dark organic soils predominate these mottles may be "masked" and unrecognizable, but they can still be there.

Soils that have a thick, dark brown or black surface horizon may also drain poorly. Some of these soils are called *peats* or *mucks*. They are usually located in bogs, depressions and areas of poor drainage. These fragile soils are poor for trail locations unless a bridge boardwalk is provided to keep hikers out of direct contact with them.

Soil Texture — Soil texture refers to the relative proportions of various sized groups of grains in a mass of soil. It is an important characteristic in the trafficability of soils. In general, loam soils with a mixture of sands, clay and silt will resist compaction and erosion most successfully. The smaller sizes of silt and clay particles add cohesion; sand and gravel are present for porosity and water absorption. These moderately sandy soils will resist compaction and will absorb a high level of rainfall, making them good for trail use.

Caution should be used when building trails across pure sand. Sand blows when dry, supports few plants for soil rentention, and can lead to a shifting treadway.

Soils made up mostly of silt and clay will be muddy when wet, cracked and dusty when dry. These soils are highly erodible and if possible should be avoided for trails, especially on steep slopes. Coarse fragments in the treadway can increase trafficability. Gravel-sized fragments imbedded in the soil matrix help to hold the more erodible sand, silt and clay particles in place. They also improve soil drainage. Loose gravel on the trail surface may cause uncertain footing, but this is not a serious limitation for a trail.

Rocks and stones, while making footing somewhat variable, are not serious limitations to trail placement either. In fact, they can be natural erosion retardants when used in a trail treadway.

Field inspection of soil texture can easily be done by feeling with the fingers. Sometimes this process is supplemented with a hand lens. Here is what to look for:

Sand — Loose, single grains, individual grains readily seen and easily felt.

Loam — A mixture of different grades of sand, silt and clay; it has a gritty feel, yet is fairly smooth and plastic.

Clay — A fine-textured soil which usually breaks into clods or lumps that are hard when dry; quite plastic and sticky when wet.

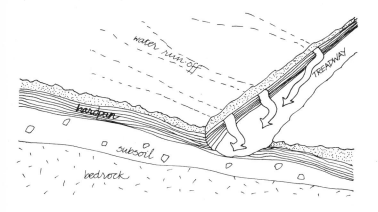

Soil Structure — The relationships between horizons and the characteristics of each horizon affect the percolation of water into soils. Many soils have hard, compacted horizons called *hardpans*. These hardpans are generally impervious to the downward movement of water. In areas where hardpans are evident, trail surfaces may become wet and soft, making them susceptible to damage.

Soil Depth — Shallow soils over bedrock or hardpan can lead to problems on hiking trails. Such soils are often heavy and saturated with water, causing them to erode quickly and slough off when walked upon. This is especially true in steep terrain, where steep rock slabs can become dangerously exposed after some wear from hiking. Hikers seeking safe passage use plantlife on the edge of the trail for handholds killing the plants and aggravating trail widening problems. This process is, in most cases, unsuitable to enjoyable hiking and disruptive to the natural enviromnent.

The limitations of soil depth are especially critical in the alpine zone. The soil mantle here is only several inches thick and plantlife is small and easily damaged by foot traffic.

In the alpine zone the maintainer must take special pains to mark the trail without any abrupt turns. In this way shortcuts are discouraged. Lining the path with rock, and in extreme cases even rockwall, will help to contain the impact of hiking traffic on thin alpine soils to a small area.

Soil depth and grade are the most important factors in determining the appropriateness of a trail location. They are both easy to measure in the field with a soil auger, by eye or with an inclinometer. Therefore, they can usually be evaluated during the initial phases of a proposed trail installation.

Rock wall along fragile Franconia Ridge, N.H. channels hiker impact. (facing page)

SUMMARY OF SOIL INDICATORS FOR EVALUATION OF A PROPOSED TRAIL INSTALLATION

Conditions	Conditions Posing Slight Limitations for Trail Installations	Conditions Posing Moderate Limitations for Trail Installations	Conditions Posing Severe Limitations for Trail Installations
Soil Wetness	Depth to seasonal high water table four feet or more; well drained to moderately well drained	Depth to seasonal high water table one to four feet; excessively drained	Depth to seasonal high water table less than one foot poorly drained
Soil Texture	Particle mixture of sand, clay, silt; 20-50% of content gravel	High sand content; less than 50% but geater than 20% of content gravel	High clay content; no gravel
Soil Structure			Hardpans less than one foot from soil surface; peaty, muck soils
Soil Depth to Bedrock	Greater than three feet	1.5 - 3 feet	Less than 1.5 feet
Slope	0 - 5%*	5 - 20%	Greater than 20%

*Slope is the number of feet of vertical rise per one hundred feet of horizontal distance, expressed as a percentage — that is, a 10% slope rises ten feet vertically for every hundred feet traversed horizontally.

Topography

Topographical variations[4] in the landscape such as hills, knolls and views are elements of a stimulating and interesting trail design. If the trail fits the lay of the land, hikers will have a greater sense of adventure and anticipation in traveling. Subtle turns and undulations in grade, steep and dramatic climbs to a view or the sudden appearance of a waterfall keep interest and personal satisfaction high.

These features of the landscape must be provided with minimum disruption and environmental degradation to soils and plantlife. Most important in this regard is the placement of trails on steep slopes. Gullying caused by trail erosion will soon develop on trails that climb long, steep gradients. Therefore, a happy medium must be found between the trail's function of gaining elevation and the tendency of water to rapidly erode trails on steep grades. This happy medium can be found with a *sidehill* trail location, so that running water will cross the trail but not run down the treadway at high velocities that can seriously aggravate erosion.

Switchbacks — When the function of the trail is to climb a long, steep grade on a mountain, sidehilling alone cannot provide the needed rise in elevation. The lateral area available for a sidehill trail is limited by terrain, so the trail must turn and start its lateral motion in the opposite direction. This turn is aptly named a *switchback*. It has been used for centuries in road and trail design.

The greatest potential for failure in switchback design is to build too many switchbacks too close together. Hikers on a trail with short switchbacks will take shortcuts,

---

[4]Much of the information in this section comes from *Guidelines for the Pacific Crest National Scenic Trail*, U. S. Department of Agriculture, 1971.

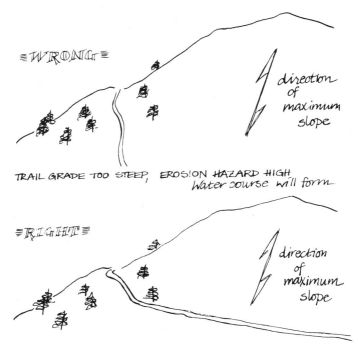

≡ WRONG ≡

direction
of
maximum
slope

TRAIL GRADE TOO STEEP, EROSION HAZARD HIGH
Water course will form

≡ RIGHT ≡

direction
of
maximum
slope

SIDEHILL TRAIL LOCATION   CONTROLS EROSION
Water crosses trail but won't flow down treadway

especially when descending. This is turn aggravates plant mortality and soil erosion, because the sidehill practice is nullified by direct, steep shortcuts. Water courses and erosion will develop on such shortcuts, especially after they become trampled by large numbers of hikers.

Long stretches between switchbacks have the added advantage of requiring that fewer be built. Switchbacks, as will be seen in the next chapter, are difficult to build so that they drain properly. Keeping them few in number holds both initial construction costs and maintenance costs to manageable levels. Also, repetition is monotonous to the hiker.

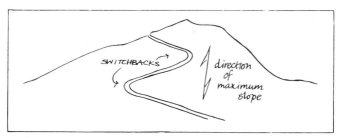

On a well-designed trail, one switchback is not visible from another. Use is made of natural topographic features, and the length of trail segments is varied to sustain interest. Steady grades give the hiker a feeling of substantial progress in climbing.

Another technique which can be used to control short-cutting past switchbacks is to make the switchback into a wide turn. In so doing you run the risk of having a small section of the turn running straight up the fall line. However, if the danger of shortcutting is great, as is the case in open hardwoods or above treeline where hikers can see great distances, then a wide turn running straight up the grade may be the best choice to make. The trail treadway on the steepest part of the turn can be hardened with soil stabilization techniques such as steps in order to keep these steep turns stable.

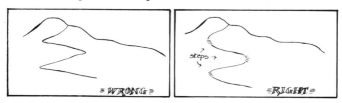

Left, *narrow switchbacks are prone to shortcutting.*
Right, *wide turns fortified with steps prevent shortcutting.*

On short, frequently used trails such as between a water supply and a campsite or a parking lot and a view, switchbacks are best not used. They are most appropriate when designed over a large area, thus permitting adequate vegetative screening between switchback legs. Short trails do not cover enough space to permit the proper design of foolproof switchbacks.

TRAILS SHOULD TAKE ADVANTAGE OF DRAMATIC TOPOGRAPHY. Care to avoid rockfall below and excess risk above must be balanced with the drama of the surroundings.

Rocks, cliffs, ledges and caves provide interest in a trail location. These rigors of the landscape should not be avoided in designing a trail. Caution should be used, however, in placing trails over shale slides or talus slopes and at cliff edges. Tree scars and talus with recent fracture surfaces are a good indication that falling rock would be unreasonably dangerous under these ledges and cliffs. Trails skirting the tops of cliffs should be clearly defined and obvious to the hiker. Wet, mossy rock and ice in the spring and fall indicate that there should be reasonably cautious use of exciting cliffside trail locations. If these limiting conditions are not serious, the trail should take every advantage of dramatic topography.

Vegetation

The type and density of vegetation in areas proposed for trail development have two primary functions in design:

1) An aesthetic function, enhancing the hiking experience, and
2) A management function, as a tool to assist the designer in protecting the environment.

Variety and diversity of vegetative communities along a trail route promote hiker interest and satisfaction, especially if the trail is proposed for environmental study, such as a nature trail. Likewise, continuity in species composition has its own special attraction: a prolonged stretch of dense woods can promote a hauntingly exciting feeling of anticipation and adventure.

Obviously there is no single criterion for making an aesthetic choice between one type of vegetative cover and another. In fact, the aesthetic quality of vegetative cover will usually be a secondary consideration. Primary emphasis in design must be placed on the characteristics of soils and topography, for these have a greater influence on trail stability in mountainous and unstable terrain.

There are several ways vegetation can be used in trail design, among them:

1) **To channel and contain hiker traffic** — Vegetation, particularly dense growth, can be used as a tool to control trail traffic. Treadway boundaries are profoundly affected by the density of trailside trees and shrubs; therefore, dense undergrowth enables greater flexibility in trail layout. For instance, switchbacks are less likely to be bypassed by over-enthusiastic hikers if dense shrubbery lines the edge of the trail. Damage to soils is therefore contained to a narrow band.

2) **To retard trail erosion** — Roots of trailside vegetation retard soil erosion on the treadway. However,

with particularly unstable soils, steep slopes and high visitor use, this root stability is not sufficient to prevent resource damage.

3) **To protect from the weather** — Experienced hikers realize the value of tree protection, especially after having descended from the alpine zone in bad weather conditions. This aspect of vegetative cover is most important to the designer in the planning and location of campsites, where protection from the elements is a requisite of good site location.

4) **To buffer and insulate hiking activities** — An increasingly important aspect of vegetation in our crowded national parks and forests is its wonderful ability to break up lines of sight and to absorb sound. Visual and acoustical buffering of incompatible activities like off-road vehicle use guarantees that a high-quality hiking experience can, if managed properly, continue to be available on a limited land base.

A good example of the ability of vegetation to buffer sound is in snowmobile trail design. Proper buffering using vegetation, hillsides and other features can reduce snowmobile sound levels by one-third to one-half. Vegetation is also a valuable buffer between a trail with high public use and a sensitive environment such as a pond shore.

5) **To provide building material** — As will be seen in Part II of this book, trailside trees are a major source of building material for treadway reconstruction. The availability of trees of suitable size for treadway hardening may be a factor in whether or not a trail is routed through fragile terrain such as a bog or marsh. Native trees for hardening keep costs low and add to the natural character of a trail.

6) **To use as indications of soil characteristics** — Accurate understanding of soil conditions in an area requires direct analysis. However, cursory examination of vegetation can indicate broad soil characteristics. Tree size and age indicate soil fertility —

large, young trees indicate deep, well drained soils while small, stunted trees correspondingly indicate marginal soil conditions.

The preponderance of a species can give clues to soil texture, depth and wetness. Pine and oak are characteristic of sand soils, while fir, spruce and hemlock indicate shallow soil depths. Swamp maple, cedar and tamarack grow in soils that are moist and boggy for much of the year.

Creative use of the vegetative character of a trail is an important part in the trail management scheme. Thoughtful design optimizes the beneficial characteristics of vegetation.

3

TRAIL LAYOUT

TRAIL LAYOUT IS REALLY ONLY PRACTICAL application of the information in Chapters 1 and 2. A good layout must satisfy recreational needs, as discussed in the first chapter, as well as being environmentally stable, as covered in the second chapter.

The most important work in a trail installation is obviously done in the field. After the initial development of a trail proposal, the route should be checked and rechecked on location. The more time spent in this layout phase, the better the trail location will be.

Use U. S. Geological Survey (USGS) topographical maps upon which all data is recorded. In particularly complex layout projects, it may be helpful to make a card file that refers back to this map. In this file all pertinent features are recorded for eventual use in the final on-the-ground layout.

Each of the cards outlines the nature of a feature and whether it has a positive or negative effect on the trail;

also included is any other pertinent information such as addresses of landowners, if for instance the particular feature is an ownership boundary on private land.

As this information file develops, each feature will become a checkpoint which must either be avoided, as in the case of a bog or a steep slope, or which will be included if its effect on the trail is positive, as would be the case with a good view. The final choice of route, then, will involve a combination of connecting positive features and circumventing negative ones.

This layout process must also pay heed to the environmental characteristics of the landscape outlined in Chapter 2. Where possible always use a sidehill trail location, for instance, and check soil characteristics at regular intervals. Keep the gradient below 20% if possible, unless trail hardening is planned during the installation.

This layout process then becomes one of trial and error. As it proceeds the designer will be constantly backtracking and reflagging the route until finally the location satisfies the requirements outlined in Chapters 1 and 2.

It may be helpful at this point to get professional assistance from different sources such as civil engineers, soil scientists and foresters who can all add their special skills to a thorough evaluation of the trail site.

A technique which may also be helpful is to talk to local people, especially the older folks who are familiar with the land. These people can be extremely helpful to the trail designer, and in many cases can point out all the significant features in a particular area, as well as give a broad and personal account of its history.

Aerial photographs can reveal even to the untrained eye such features as ledges, water courses, old logging roads potentially useable for the trail, and other detailed information on the land's characteristics. These aerial photos are available from the USDA's Soil Conservation

Service, or in the case of parks and forests from the managing agencies involved.

The trail route should be flagged with engineer's flagging tape. The color should be bright enough to stand out, and should not be the same as the prevailing colors of the fall foliage if the layout is to be done in that season. (For example, don't use yellow flagging tape in a beechwood forest in the fall.) The flagging should be placed at fairly close intervals and it should be tied securely on living trees and their branches. If the flag line has to last through a winter don't count on having a long, loose tail on a flag. It will blow off. The best technique is to tie the flag tightly around the trunk of a tree.

The best time of year to do trail layout is during the spring and fall, when the leaves are off the trees and the ground is clear of ice and snow.

If there is time, it is beneficial to check a trail location at several different times of the year. Checking it in winter, for instance, enables the designer to know if the trail is also appropriate for ski touring. Checking it in the spring gives an indication of drainage and wetness problems.

All of this work requires that the designer be a good outdoorsman. Skilled knowledge of map and compass, sa well as demanding orienteering in a trailless area, are requirements for the job.

Trail layout is both safer and easier if the work is done by pairs. If one person stays stationary on one of the checkpoints and calls to the other, efficient layout is facilitated.

4

TRAIL CLEARING

Trailman clears trail high to avoid snags on packs and to allow for branches becoming lowered with rain and snow. (facing page)

THE INFORMATION PRESENTED UP TO THIS point has been oriented toward building a new trail. This second part of the book discusses the needs of existing trails that, because of increased popularity, have become damaged or worn to an unacceptable degree. Standard trail techniques for clearing and marking are included. Most existing trail clubs and the systems they maintain face the conditions on trails that will be addressed here.

One of the most important jobs for trail maintainers is clearing established trails. Without a regular clearing even frequently used trails can dissolve in just four or five years into a netherworld of overgrowth.

The backbone of most trail organizations is their ability to provide the public with a clear trail using a consistent, long-term annual maintenance program. Such a program goes farthest in the total maintenance effort to make a trail or trail system satisfying for foot travel.

The actual techniques for keeping trails clear will vary with the environment of the trail and with the amounts and types of visitor use the trail receives. Also, different maintainers develop and use different techniques suitable for their particular tasks and based on their individual preferences. Favorite tools and techniques can vary widely in different areas, among different organizations and even among members of the same crew. The point here is to find the best methods for you and your organization. This chapter outlines the essential information needed to understand and execute a trail clearing project.

Before clearing East Link on Old Speck.

Standards

A well-cleared trail is one upon which a large hiker with a big pack can walk erect without touching limbs, trees or brush. Footing is clear and the trail is easy to follow because the line of sight, both forward and back, is open and unobstructed. Branches of trailside shrubs, weighted down in wet weather and snow (if it is a winter trail), will not obscure the trail.

Width — The proper width for a cleared trail varies with terrain and vegetation. A four to eight foot clear-

After clearing East Link on Old Speck.

ance suffices in most situations. In thick growth a three foot clearance may be most practical and possibly even desirable, if it provides a pleasant tunnel effect.

In high-use areas and on steep slopes with thin, unstable soils, a narrow trail may be desirable to stabilize soils with the roots of trailside trees, shrubs and grasses. It should be noted, however, that leaving trails narrow is a limited palliative; unstable soils on sloping trails under heavy user pressure will deteriorate regardless of how narrow they are. A narrow treadway can contain trampling, though, and therefore reduce hiker impact on soils by containing it to a narrow area.

Height — Normally a trail is cleared to a height of eight feet, or as high as one can reach. On slopes, members of the crew can stand uphill from their work, bringing high branches more easily into reach. Where trees are large enough, a canopy should be left over the trail. This will help shade shrubs, weeds and grasses, dampening their usually prolific growth. Correspondingly, one can enable wildflowers to grow by clearing back the canopy to let in sunlight. This can be done selectively to minimize the "highway" appearance of excessive clearing. In the case of a trail that is popular in winter, the maintainer may want to clear it particularly high. This will enable easier travel when snow up to three or four feet deep lies on the ground. This high clearing can be done in the summer with special tools such as pole pruner or pole saw. However, it can perhaps be more easily accomplished with a winter trail clearing session.

Patrolling

Patrolling is annual maintenance done early in the hiking season to remove winter blowdown damage from hiking trails. In this way trails are open for heavy use early in the hiking season, complaints are reduced and additional work for later in the season can be carefully studied. Covering trails early in the year also gives maintainers good exercise in preparation for strenuous work later in the maintenance season.

Patrolling is best done in pairs with the workers leap-frogging from blowdown to blowdown, enabling them to patrol significant distances per day.

The standards already described for width and height can be applied to blowdown removal. In the most common situation a blowdown lies across the axis of a trail within six feet of the ground. This type of blowdown usually requires two cuts, one on each edge of the trail, with the center piece being removed and discarded off to the side.

Other situations the patroller will meet include trees that have fallen right down the trail or trees whose tops have broken off and hang down onto the trail. Removal of these blowdowns can be time consuming — the tree has to be cut into manageable pieces and rolled or carried off the trail. Often a "leaner" has to be cut first to drop it into the trail and then cut into pieces for removal.

In certain situations blowdowns are best left in place. In areas with chronic problems from off-road vehicle intrusions, blowdowns can help to discourage travel. Blowdowns lying directly on the trail do not impede progress as much as those that are situated higher; therefore, because of a heavy work load or because there is a need for heavier tools, a step-up notch can be cut and the tree left for later removal. With particularly big trees a single cut and displacement of the resulting pieces will provide the clearance needed for hiking.

Standardizing

Standardizing is the technique of clearing brush next to a trail to put it into standard condition, which means that there should be adequate clearance in width and height for comfortable hiking.

Low shrubs and young trees are cut close to the ground to prevent tripping, and to keep stumps from sprouting. This low growth should be removed back to the outside edge of the cleared trail. Annual growth such as ferns can be left to die later in the summer and fall unless it is particularly thick and aggravating.

Special attention should be paid to small softwoods and to the lateral branches of larger softwoods. Their needles become wet on a misty mountain day, and if brushed they get hikers quickly and surprisingly wet.

Brush should be cut flush with the stem. Stubs are ugly and they can create bothersome and sometimes dangerous snags for packs and clothing. Branches growing toward the trail should be cut back to the next limb growing away from the trail. If trees are pruned in this way rather than being indiscriminately chopped, sucker growth will be reduced. A root system geared to provide nutrients to a tree of a certain size will cause aggravated growth in the remainder of the tree if a large part is removed. By leaving growth directed away from the trail, future maintenance efforts can be reduced.

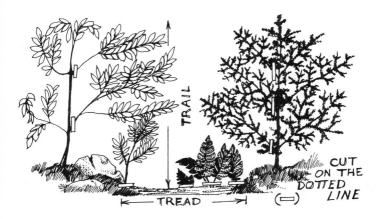

TRAIL

TREAD

CUT
ON THE
DOTTED
LINE

(▭)

If a short treetop has to be removed, it is generally better to remove the whole tree, since removal of the terminal buds will aggravate lateral growth into the trail. Removal of the whole tree, or at least cutting all lateral branches, is the second best option — still better than cutting off the top of the tree only.

Special situations such as the following require special consideration:

1) *Alpine Trails* — Judgment and temperance should be used when clearing trails near or above treeline where the climate is severe and growth rates are very slow. Trees three to four feet tall can be sixty or seventy years old. Small trees and shrubs at treeline grow in interdependent communities called *krummholz*. Removal of one tree in a patch of krummholz can jeopardize the other trees in the patch, which join roots and branches in protection against wind and cold. It is necessary to develop one's sense of growth units by analyzing which plants are influencing and perhaps maintaining cover for delicate and desirable flora.

2) *Timber harvesting* — All too frequently trail maintainers on private land find that a timber oper-

ation has to cut across the trail. Clean-up and re-opening of the trail involves locating and flagging the trail, then removing all slash and debris. This requires a lot of work.

Clean-up

A good clearing job can be completely nullified if all branches and debris are not completely removed from the trail. One person on the crew should be responsible for clean-up. He picks up all branches, trees and debris and scatters them clear of the trail. Piles should be avoided because they are unsightly and can create a fire hazard. The trail treadway should be raked with a lawn rake to ensure complete clean-up and unobstructed footing. Downed trees are best dragged butt first until the top is completely off the trail. This will also serve to conceal the tree from hikers. Large limbs and small trees can be thrown clear of the trail, provided that they do not hang in the branches of shrubs and trees next to the trail or stick up butt first.

5

TRAIL MARKING

TRAILS MUST BE MARKED in an understandable, systematic and vandalproof manner. This can be done with a variety of techniques, the principle ones being paint blazing, signs and for treeless areas, cairns.

Paint Blazing

The most effective technique[5] for marking a hiking trail is with paint. Its durability and universal availability make it clearly the most practical method for marking most hiking trails.

The standard blaze on the Appalachian Trail is a white two by six inch mark placed on trees and rocks.

---

[5]A portion of this material was developed from the *Trail Manual for the Appalachian Trail* published by the Appalachian Trail Conference. This publication is recommended for additional information on paint blazing.

The shape of this blaze has proven to be a good, easily spotted one for trail marking, so it is recommended for use on other trails.

Along any trail the blazing should be consistent for its entire length. Changing the frequency of blazes can cause hikers confusion. Likewise, there should be no gaps in the marking; blazing should be uninterrupted.

Paint blazing must be neat. Clean, neat, well-placed blazes improve a trail. Indiscriminate splotches can seriously detract from the hiker's appreciation of his surroundings.

In the installation of a new trail or trail system, or in the installation of new markings on an old trail, a well-planned standard should be developed. Color, frequency, placement and form should be carefully thought out before installation so that changes do not have to be made later. The best colors to use are blue, red, highway yellow, white and orange. One may wish to develop a primary color for a main trail in a system and have a secondary color for side trails. This is the procedure used along the Appalachian Trail. The main route is marked in white, with side trails in blue.

Care should be used when the trail is located next to private land boundary lines. Boundaries are usually marked with paint and if the theme color of a trail is the same used on boundaries in the trail's vicinity, confusion can result. Landowner relationships will also be aggravated.

Water-based paints are the easiest to handle and apply; they also dry quickly. Outdoor latex or lucite is sufficient. These paints will not last long if the surface is not thoroughly dry, however. Therefore, if the weather is wet, do not mark trails. Longer lasting paints such as enamels may be desirable if the trail is infrequently maintained.

Blazes are placed in both fore and aft directions to indicate the route of travel both ways. They should be placed on trees or rocks which "strike the eye" while traveling along the trail. A large tree is preferable to a small one. A good way to determine the tree on which to place a blaze is to face down the trail ahead as one finishes painting a blaze and note quickly the tree at a suitable distance which catches the eye. Walk toward that tree and if it is not too far off the trail, place the next blaze on it. On a straight, wide or well-cleared trail this may well be far ahead. One well-placed blaze is more effective than several improperly located ones. Bear in mind that intervening branches and leaves that droop under rain or snow may obscure vision between blazes unless they are cleared away. Summer growth may be surprising in this respect.

The frequency of paint blazes will be determined by the character of the trail. On narrow woods trails, blazes should be *visible from each other*. On well-worn roads blazes may be spaced farther apart, depending on the nature of the terrain. A good guide is that the hiker should never have to walk more than one hundred paces without being able to see a blaze either ahead or behind him.

To make a blaze quickly and properly after the spot selected has been prepared with a scraper or wire brush, a one-inch brush is dipped in the paint, drawn out lightly against the rim of the can and held nearly level so the paint on the upper side will not spill. With the brush held straight the end is placed flat against the tree at the top of the blaze, drawn quickly and firmly down, then the handle turned up and an upstroke made. The brush is lifted just before the top of the blaze is reached. In this way the brush spreads just enough to make a two-inch blaze, and the top and bottom of the blaze are straight across. Ordinarily nothing more needs to be done, aside from touching up the edges or corners if the paint did not "take" evenly, or filling in crevices on a rough-barked tree.

From time to time it becomes necessary to obliterate paint blazes. The reason for this may be extensive relocation of a section of trail, a slight change due to some recent obstruction such as beaver flowage, recent growth which has obstructed the view of a blaze, or the necessity of standardizing the marking of a trail section which has been improperly marked. In renewing blazes it is almost always necessary to obliterate portions of old blazes which have been widened by tree growth.

To obliterate unwanted blazes or standardize blazes expanded by tree growth a neutralizing paint is used. This should be brown or grey paint matched to the surface being covered. If the trees are mostly conifers, a yellow-brown is best. When the trees are mostly hardwoods, a red-brown is satisfactory.

When the trail is relocated, all blazes on the abandoned section should be obliterated. It is not sufficient to obliterate those at either end. Persons straying from the trail or bushwhacking through the woods for any reason may find the old trail route, see such blazes, assume they are on the trail and be greatly misled, possibly with unfortunate results. (There have been such cases, resulting in criticism of the maintaining group involved.)

Immediately beyond any crossing road or trail there must be a trail indication blaze even though there is also a directional sign. Because of the possibility that this blaze may disappear due to road clearing, it is advisable to have a second or safety blaze at a near distance, perhaps from fifty to a hundred feet beyond the crossing. This serves as insurance if the primary marking of the crossing is obliterated.

Do not fail to mark the trail because of the thought that no one could possibly get lost in that area. Conditions may be unexpectedly changed by new trail or road construction, lumbering or blowdowns resulting from storms. Under such circumstances, blazes at infrequent intervals may result in difficulty in following the trail.

It should be borne in mind that trail marking is for the benefit of one who is unfamiliar with the terrain; this consideration must be *the guiding principle* for one who thoroughly knows the terrain.

At important changes in the route, such as turns into a less-defined trail or road, there should be two disconnected blazes of the prescribed size, one two inches above the other and placed like the regular blazes at right angles to the trail. This symbol serves as a warning to the hiker: "Stop . . . Look!" It does not indicate the direction of the turn. Single and double blazes are the only symbols adopted by the Appalachian Trail Conference for the Appalachian Trail.

To ensure adequate and proper spacing, it is desirable when possible for blazing to be treated as a separate job for each hiking direction — that is, blazes should be painted in one direction at a time. Where possible avoid placing blazes on both sides of the same tree, since the loss of one tree will otherwise result in a two-fold loss in marking.

Paint should not be applied until the surface of the tree has been prepared. The area on which the blaze is to be placed should be scraped, not cut. To do this, a hardwood floor scraper such as the Red Devil Scraper is satisfactory. The size with a 2½ inch blade and a six inch handle is most efficient. Usually two or three downward strokes are sufficient.

Preparation of a rock surface can be done with a wire brush. Vigorous rubbing will remove lichens and mosses, making the surface more suitable for paint application.

The tree surface should be prepared for a painting using a hardwood floor scraper.

Signs

Signs are an essential component of any trail. The trail's name, direction, highlights, distances and destina-

After the surface has been prepared, the paint can easily be applied.

tion all need to be conveyed to the hiker using them. Several different types of signs are discussed in this section, along with information on their fabrication, installation and maintenance.

Wooden Routed Signs — The most popular and attractive signs for hiking trails are made of wood with the lettering cut into the sign with a *router*. These signs are used extensively in our national parks and forests. Because of their attractiveness they are sometimes taken by souvenir hunters and vandals; however, if they are properly hung they should last many years. Because the lettering is actually cut into the wood, the sign will be legible even after all paint has been worn off by weathering.

Fabrication of Wooden Routed Signs — The fabrication of a routed wooden sign is a time-consuming process that requires skill and patience. However, any person with an artistic bent and the proper equipment can make professional-looking signs using this method.

Type of Wood — The choice of wood to be used should take into account characteristics such as workability, durability and strength, as well as availability and cost. The best woods are clear-heart redwood, basswood, Ponderosa yellow pine, white pine or western fir. In the southeastern United States cypress and locust are often used. Get good quality stock, straight and free of knots.

Size of Sign Board — Boards one inch thick are appropriate for most routed wooden signs. At trailheads where large descriptive signs are needed, two-inch-thick stock may be more appropriate. The length and width of the sign varies with the length of the message and with its importance. Trailhead signs may be as large as two by three feet, whereas directional arrows can be as small as three by eight inches. Because of our large highway signs there may be a tendency to make trail signs large also; however, this is not necessary because hikers stand directly in front of a trail sign. Therefore, except for the sign at the roadside trailhead, signs should be kept small. Particularly large trailhead signs can be made from several boards joined with dowel joints or a similar wood-joining technique.

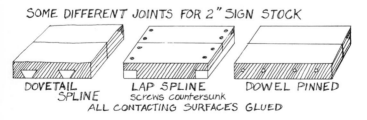

SOME DIFFERENT JOINTS FOR 2" SIGN STOCK

DOVETAIL SPLINE   LAP SPLINE   DOWEL PINNED
                      screws countersunk
          ALL CONTACTING SURFACES GLUED

Size of Lettering — Most signs will not need lettering larger than 1½ inches in height. This large lettering is used for the name of a trail, and is usually placed at the upper end of the sign face. The text of the sign can then be conveyed with lettering ½ inch or ¾ inch in height.

Stencils — Stencils should be used when laying out the text of a sign. They can be bought from a sign manu-

facturer, but are fairly expensive from this source. It may be better to visit the local stationery or art supply store. Many of them sell inexpensive stencils for tracing letters of different sizes.

Routing — After a sign has had its text laid out in pencil, the letters should be routed. Practice on scrap

wood to get the best results on the sign board. Considerable skill is needed to get professional results. Practice will make perfect.

A sharp bit is essential to good lettering. A dull bit will leave "feathers" that are ugly, particularly after they are painted. A dull bit will also burn the wood.

A carbide-tipped bit, V-shaped or U-shaped, should be used. Carbide steel is extremely hard and will last a long time if used with care. If a V-shaped bit is used then it can be either raised or lowered when routing different-sized letters. If U-shaped bits are used then different bits will have to be purchased for the different-sized letters.

If the router bit is used on plywood it may be irreparably damaged because of the hard glue used to join the layers of the plywood. Always wear safety goggles when using a router.

Painting — As with blazing, colors for signs should be carefully chosen so that they will not have to be changed at some future date. Two colors are used, one for the background and one for the lettering. Most park and

forest areas use a brown background with a white, cream or yellow letter. This color scheme blends in well with the natural qualities of a trail.

The sign background can either be stained with an oil stain and then varnished with a good spar varnish or it can be painted with an outdoor latex. Two or three coats are recommended. After the background is painted, the lettering is done. Great patience should be used when painting the letters. It would be a shame to ruin a sign in its final stages. The letters should be filled with paint rather than painted. This will give the letters an attractive "liquid" look. Small artist's brushes are needed for this part of the sign's fabrication.

Hanging a Sign — Most signs at trail junctions are best hung on trees. If nails are used then holes slightly smaller than the diameter of the nail should be drilled in the face of the sign. The nails should protrude a bit after installation. This way they will not split the sign or be forced through it as the tree grows. Galvanized nails prevent unsightly rust stains on the face of the sign.

Because of the attractiveness of routed wooden signs, they are frequently stolen. Hanging such a sign with

nails does not offer a thief much resistance; therefore, another more durable method is recommended. Use a sign backing spiked with long ring spikes to the tree. The sign board is then bolted to the backing with rust-proof zinc-plated bolts and washers. The backing can be made from scrap lumber from any building operation. Using a sign backing also protects the sign from splitting from tree growth. If this method of hanging is anticipated early enough, the location of the bolt and washer can be planned with the location of the letters in the text of the sign in mind.

The most attractive and effective method of hanging signs is to use a sign post. A post should be used at the trailhead and on popular trails getting heavy use. A ten-inch diameter post seven feet long and buried to a depth of three feet will usually suffice.

The upper end of the post should be beveled with an axe. At the base of the post a threaded rod or reinforcing steel can be placed in a hole drilled at right angles to its center to prevent vandals from turning or removing the sign and post.

The post should be treated. The base is best treated with a good wood preservative like Osmosplastic. The top of the post can be painted.

The sign should be attached to the post on a flattened, counter sunk surface. The sign can be bolted to the post using a socket wrench with long $\frac{3}{8}$ inch lag bolts counter-sunk into the surface of the sign. If these countersunk surfaces are filled with plastic wood, removal of the sign becomes that much more difficult.

Master Sign List — A master sign list for a trail system should be developed by the maintainer. This list documents the locations of all signs, the text of each and the size of each sign board. With a system such as this, maintenance, repair and replacement are facilitated. Reports of missing or stolen signs are all the maintainer then needs to build a replacement.

Temporary Signs — If routed signs are not ready when a trail is to be opened, or if an important sign is stolen, a temporary sign must be erected in its place. Heavy white posterboard and permanent ink can be used to make a good temporary sign. The finished product can be encased in contact paper to waterproof the sign. Such a sign, stapled and glued to plywood and hung on a tree, should easily last one to two years. It should be checked for fading and damage from squirrels and birds if it must serve longer than that.

Stenciled Signs — A purposefully ugly sign may be the best choice in areas with vandalism problems. Metal or wooden signs painted with stenciled letters are appropriate here. Vandalism can also be reduced by placing a sign high on a tree (but not so high as to be unreadable), or by covering the back of the sign with axle grease, making firm holds on the sign difficult and unpleasant.

Cairns

Marking trails in treeless areas requires the construction of conspicuous rock piles known as *cairns*. Cairns make attractive and natural trail markers that are effective year-round because of their visibility even under the snow and ice conditions of winter. Well-placed and well-built cairns also help to protect the fragile soils of alpine areas by keeping people on a single trail. Cairns are especially important when the weary traveller must find his way in the poor visibility of an alpine storm.

Cairns should be between fifty and a hundred feet apart and should be placed along trails that have been laid out in a fairly direct fashion. People will shortcut sharp turns; therefore, it is best to keep the trail curving with the land in gentle undulations. Such trails take the easiest route, and therefore represent the most likely choice of travel for the average hiker, who is typically committed to economizing on the effort it takes to traverse ridgecrest land.

Cairns should be placed in conspicuous locations. A knoll is obviously a better location than a hollow. If a ledge or mound is available, then the cairn has greater visibility if placed on it. Occasionally light-colored rocks can be found and used at the top of a cairn, making it more visible. Occasionally painting the upper rock of a cairn will increase visibility. Paint blazes may sometimes be used in conjunction with cairns, especially in areas where rock for cairn building is scarce.

FIRST LAYER

SECOND;
note, joints of 1ST
layer are bridged
by second stones

A WELL MADE CAIRN; rocks lean
toward center, and joints are
broken.

Construction of Cairns — Cairns should be built to a height of four or five feet. They should be fairly squat, almost as wide at the base as they are high. Cairns constructed in this manner effectively resist weathering and tampering by hikers.

Occasionally cairns have to be smaller when rock for construction is unavailable. Care should be used in quarrying rock in areas with thin soil mantles because of the potential damage to these fragile areas. In some cases it will be better not to use cairns at all, but to depend on wooden posts and paint blazes.

Large, flat rocks should be used, especially for the base layer. The upper surfaces of the rocks in each layer should all slope toward the center of the cairn. If this method is used for each succeeding tier, then gravity will tend to stablize the cairn's construction in much the same way that a stone arch is strengthened by a keystone.

Each stone placed on a cairn should have at least three points of contact. Then each rock placed will be stable and will not wiggle. Wedging small stones into cracks between large rocks is not a good practice. Each stone should be stabilized with its neighbor stones. In this way a good, strong cairn can be built.

Marking Systems

There is a growing need for development of a widely recognized mark for hiking trails. Different trail groups in different states are grappling with various experimental techniques. Plastic diamonds, metal arrows and different quality paints are all being evaluated.

This process is a good one and should be accelerated. The hiking trail constituency needs a symbol that will be widely recognized and accepted by all users of trail lands, including landowners, off-road vehicle and hikers. With a standard mark recognizable by the people in a community, the trail will be more widely accepted as a facility that is an essential part of it.

6

GUIDELINES FOR TRAIL
RECONSTRUCTION

ALL LAND AREAS HAVE AN INHERENT and variable ability to sustain recreational use without suffering damage to soils, vegetation and water. This ability can be relatively low, especially in mountain parks and forests with steep slopes and abundant water run-off. To increase this land ability to withstand hiking use without resource damage, trail management programs need to be introduced.

The intensity, and consequently the expense, of management of a satisfying and undamaged trail environment is controlled basically by two factors. The first is the volume of use an area receives. As use increases there is more wear and tear on a trail, and therefore the need for increased trail stabilization work is present if soils and plantlife are to be maintained in a healthy condition. The second factor governing management is the character of the land itself. Areas that are wet, located on steep slopes, characterized by poor soils, or which support fragile vegetation such as that present in the alpine

zone require particularly careful — and sometimes costly — management. There are management techniques which allow a certain degree of use in such areas, but the associated costs of labor and materials will be high and an inevitable loss of natural qualities will result. Trails in these more sensitive areas should be avoided if possible, or at least minimized.

When to Relocate

Gullies or wide muddy areas on trails can be tackled in one of two ways: they can be circumnavigated with a relocated section of trail or they can be hardened with the proven techniques described later. When deliberating on this choice, two questions should be answered:

1) *Will the new section of trail have the same environmental conditions and the same design as the damaged section being replaced?*

Often the answer to this question is "yes", which means that the same steep slope or boggy soils have to be traversed by the relocated section of the trail. If this is the case then more often than not it is best to stick to the old location rather than open up a new one that will deteriorate in the same fashion. If, however, the same terrain is crossed but in a less direct fashion — i.e., if there is a design change whereby the trail crosses the slope rather than climbs directly up it — then the relocation is probably worth considering. The same environmental conditions may predominate, but the trail design in this case is more topographically sound.

2) *Will the old section of the trail be too difficult to close?*

If the section of trail being replaced is the most obvious location in a given landscape — for example on a pond shore or on a pronounced ridge — then hikers naturally tend to assume its existence and will use the trail even after a relocation has been installed and the section in question has been closed. In these cases again it is best to stick to the old location. Sometimes in situations like this a relocation can actually hasten environmental degradation by becoming confused with the old location so that hikers begin using both routes interchangeably. When this happens there can be many problems with both locations, as well as the unplanned crossover trails that will develop because of hikers' confusion.

Generally relocations should only be used when there can be a substantial improvement in the environmental conditions on the new section. This assumes that the relocation will replace a substantial piece of trail. Short relocations around a wet area may be appropriate, but the best long-term solution is usually to either close and replace a long trail section or to reconstruct it. More often than not the hardening alternative is the best one; it will be addressed in the next two chapters.

Building Materials for Reconstruction

The techniques described here require that the trail maintainer find native materials in the vicinity of the trail and move them to the treadway for use in its reconstruction. This laborious process should be undertaken carefully and foresightfully to minimize damage to the trail environment and to maximize the quality of reconstruction.

The materials, usually wood or rock, are either cut or dug from sites near the trail but out of sight from it. This is a primary criterion in choosing reconstruction materials — that they be unnoticed and subtle in terms of what the trail user senses as he traverses a trail's length.

Wood Materials — Usually a stand of trees appropriate in size and length can be found uphill and out of sight of the trail. After the trees are cut down they should be limbed, peeled and cut to appropriate length on site so that bark, wood chips and other waste products are not left on the trail itself. Once prepared they can be hand-carried to the trail.

Rock Materials — Rock materials, more than wood, have to be found wherever they are available. Preferably they would be out of sight; however, because they leave no large and obvious traces behind, such as a tree stump does, the maintainer can use greater latitude in harvesting rock materials for trail work. Frequently, rock right next to the trail can be used, in which case dead brush and other forest litter can be placed in any hole, left by removal of the rock. Take care not to use bedrock or ledge; in addition to being hard to cut, a lasting scar may remain.

Soil for Fill — Occasionally a hole needs to be dug to provide soil for fill work along the trail. A soil pit or fill hole should be dug in these cases. Though such pits can be near the trail they should be out of direct view, and after being used they should be filled with wood debris and hidden.

Service Trails — In major construction projects it is best to gather building materials in several locations and

Service Trail

then transport them to the trail using several limited access routes. In this manner damage to surrounding areas is reduced by being contained to feeder trails which, after construction, can be closed.

Rock Work

Often the trail maintainer is confronted with an obvious solution to a classic trail problem, but because of sparse tree growth or lack of rock, building materials of adequate dimensions cannot be secured. To solve this problem there are specialized techniques which, with the proper equipment, can be used to develop rock building materials from scanty resources.

Bedrock or large boulders can be split into manageable pieces using a gas-powered *jackhammer*. Two kinds are commercially available and both are designed to be used in remote locations. The unit plus gasoline and accessories can be packed into remote locations to split rock for crews.

The Pionjar and Cobra hammers are made in Sweden. See the tool listing in Chapter 9 for suppliers. These hammers are used to drill holes in rock along its grain. (Rock, like wood, has grain — i.e., an axis plane along which there is a natural weakness.)

Jackhammer Use

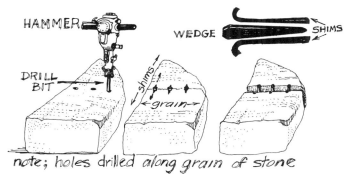

note; holes drilled along grain of stone

Shims are placed along the sides of each hole in the rock being split and wedges are placed between the shims. These are alternately driven with a three-pound sledgehammer until the rock splits.

With practice, patience and a good supply of suitable rock, a two-man team can easily provide material for a building crew.

The jackhammer can also be used to anchor steel bars or pipe for steps, signposts, railings or hand and foot loops of reinforcing rod on steep ledges. Reinforcing rod, coordinated in size with drill bit diameters, can be anchored into rock using a special hydraulic cement that expands when it dries, securing the steel in the ledge. Discretion should be used in these situations because trails that are so steep they require artificial aids such as railings and hand and foot loops may not be well suited for popular foot trails.

The hammer can also be used to remove rocks too big to haul by hand. This can be helpful if large boulders impede trail travel. Still another function of this versatile tool is its ability to cut steps into ledge that is otherwise too steep for a trail. Cut steps eliminate the need for artificial aids such as metal bars and loops; they are more natural than steel and are maintenance free.

When installing rock that has been split from a larger rock with a jackhammer, it is beneficial to put the split side down and out of sight. The drill holes are unsightly and can detract from the appearance of the trail.

Moving Large Rock — Occasionally it is helpful to be able to move rocks that weigh 300 to 400 pounds or more. For situations such as these, *cable jacks* or *come-alongs and chains* can be used to raise and lower large rocks on a slope. Tire chains wrapped around a rock are a good way to attach the come-along to it. Needless to say, this work can be dangerous, and safety should be the crew leader's main consideration. Trails receiving this kind of attention might best be closed for the duration of the reconstruction project.

Felling a Tree

One of the most demanding techniques the maintainer will have to master is that needed for felling a tree. Tree cutting is a skill that can be improved even after years of practice.

The inexperienced cutter should learn on small-diameter trees; he will learn fastest if he has instruction from someone with experience. With practice the novice can graduate to larger-diameter trees and to more complex cuts that require much pre-planning and forethought.

Several factors must be considered in order to fell a tree in the direction desired:

1) *The direction and strength of the wind* — It is easiest to fell a tree downwind or at right angles to a mild wind. It is hardest to fell a tree into a strong wind.

2) *The lean of the tree* — It is easiest to fell a tree in the direction it is leaning or at right angles to the lean. With big trees, particularly hardwoods, it can be difficult to determine the lean. The cutter has to study the tree carefully and try to determine the relative weights of the major limbs.

3) *Other trees in the area* — Great care should be used when felling to ensure that a tree does not get hung up halfway down in a neighboring tree. A hung-up tree can be very troublesome and, when he tries to get it down, potentially very dangerous to the cutter. The safest way to get a hung-up tree down is to drag the butt back from the direction of the fall. In choosing the direction for felling, ideally space will be available so that the tree will fall all the way to the ground.

Woodsman studies tree carefully before executing the back cut that will complete felling operation.

Safety Procedures — There are several rules of safe felling which should always be followed:

    1) The tree should be carefully studied to determine if it has any dead limbs that could break off during the cutting. In logging terminology these are called

"widow makers," and for obvious reasons trees with these limbs should also be avoided.

2) The area around the base of the tree should be thoroughly cleared so that the cutter will not be restricted, confined or have his concentration disturbed during the cut.

TRIM OUT THE PUCKERBRUSH

3) An exit route away from the direction of the fall should be cleared, and its use should be rehearsed several times so that in the event that something unpredictable happens the cutter can move quickly out of the danger area. This escape route will also be used after the tree starts its fall. If the fall line of the tree is uncertain then more than one escape route should be prepared. Once the tree starts to fall, the cutter should get out of the vicinity of the cut because of the danger of "kickback" from the butt of the tree.

The Cut — The first cut in a tree to be felled is the *scarf*, which is on the side of the trunk in the direction of the planned fall line. The scarf depth should be one-fifth to one-half the diameter of the trunk. If no heart rot is evident, a deeper scarf will better guarantee that the tree falls in a predictable manner.

Proper preparation of the scarf ensures a predictable fall line. The scarf should be a perfect "V" shape with no wood chips left at the point of the "V". Any wood chips left will tend to wedge the tree off the planned fall line. The fall line will be exactly at right angles to the back of the scarf, all other factors being equal.

After preparation of the scarf, the *back cut* is begun. At this time it is wise to check to make sure no fellow workers are in the vicinity of the fall line. Those in the area should be aware of the progress of the cut. Also, it is a good practice to check escape routes one final time before proceeding.

The back cut should be slightly higher than the scarf. In this way the tree will fall in the direction of the scarf.

As the back cut is made a "hinge" will be formed from the remaining wood between the scarf and the back cut. As the cutter finishes the back cut he should watch for

the first, almost imperceptible movement of the tree. If it is in the desired direction he can proceed. Minor adjustments in the direction of fall can be made by cutting the side of the hinge opposite the direction of fall desired. For example, if the tree begins to twist to the right, the cutter would deepen the back cut in the left side.

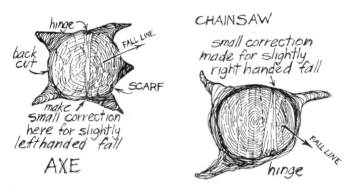

As soon as the fall begins, the cutter should immediately leave the scene along one of the pre-planned escape routes. Tree butts frequently kick back; the cutter must avoid this.

Woodsman begins to back away as tree falls.

7

EROSION CONTROL

THE MOST DIFFICULT TASK IN MAINTAINING trails over steep, mountainous terrain is establishing a stable soil situation on popular routes. In the chapter on soils and topography the problem was addressed in terms of the initial layout of the trail. The merits of relocation in areas that exhibit poor trail design and layout have also been discussed. Now we will look at the techniques that are needed to "reconstruct" and maintain a healthy soil situation on established and popular mountain trails. The techniques outlined here and in subsequent chapters are the workaday techniques used by the AMC trail crew.

Waterbars and *steps* are the two main weapons the trail maintainer has in his erosion control arsenal. Waterbars can be considered a dynamic form of erosion control and steps a static form. The maintainer should keep in mind that these are not only erosion control techniques, but also erosion preventative techniques; in other words,

trails should be waterbarred as a preventative measure, even if erosion is not yet evident.

Waterbars, set at an angle across the trail, direct the water off the trail, whereas steps, set perpendicular to the trail, serve to slow the water down and to retain soil, keeping it from washing downhill.

Tools needed for building waterbars and steps include a single bit axe, mattock and small bow saw. Waterbars should always be peeled to inhibit rot and prevent insect damage; therefore, a peeler or bark spud, which will greatly facilitate peeling should also be available. If using rock, a ten to twelve pound crowbar and a shovel are needed in addition to a mattock. An old axe or pruner for cutting roots expedites digging.

Wood Waterbars

Any rot-resistent type of wood can be used for a waterbar. Usually the maintainer has to use what is readily available. Spruce and fir are the usual choices in the northeast, as they can be cut and peeled easily and are relatively lightweight and easily carried. Hardwood can also be good, but in the large dimensions required for good waterbars they are very difficult to hand carry. Conifers such as hemlock, fir, spruce and cedar also tend to be a good deal more rot-resistant than common hardwoods such as beech or birch.

The diameter of a waterbar should be at least six to eight inches at the log's small end. The length depends on the width of the trail, which in some cases can be more than ten feet. It should extend past the outside edge of the treadway on both sides. Neither water nor people should be able to go around either end of the bar; otherwise, channeling and soil compaction will misdirect water and nullify the waterbar's purpose.

Ideally, water should be channeled from the trail without its flow being significantly impeded, thereby prevent-

A TOO-SHORT BAR WOULD ALLOW THE WATER TO TAKE THIS PATH

BE SURE THE WATERBAR FULLY REMOVES THE WATER SO THAT IT CANNOT FIND ITS WAY BACK ONTO THE TRAIL

ing it from dropping its load of sediment and clogging the bar. For this reason, natural turns in the trail can be excellent waterbar locations because the bar can remove water without deflecting it at all. A bar in this situation will be self-cleaning, an important factor in considering locations.

THE TRAIL TAKES THE TURN

AND THE WATER GOES STRAIGHT

Waterbars may tend to misdirect hikers, especially on corners. Barricading with dead brush will properly direct hikers who might be lead astray by water channels. A sign can be considered if the problem is chronic.

Once the water is well off the trail, placement of log and rock impediments should be considered to slow the water down and remove its energy without damaging trailside soils. This is especially important if water falls or drops steeply off the trail. A rock, like an object placed at the base of a gutter on a house, should be used in this situation; otherwise, erosion undermining the lower side of the trail might be a problem. In the alpine zone where plants are small and easily disturbed, this can be a particularly vexing situation.

Water Runoff

Placement — The first and most important step in the construction of a waterbar is deciding where it should be placed. Only by thoroughly planning placement, angle and length will the maintainer build an effective waterbar.

On a steep slope where erosion is occurring, water must be removed at the top of the slope before damage can occur. Usually a combination of steps and waterbars are used, though if soils are quite stable and slopes are not steep then waterbars alone may be all that is necessary.

Spacing depends on the steepness of slope and the availability of places to divert the water off the trail. In a gully or on a poorly laid-out section of trail, placement choices are usually few in number. On grades of 20% or more, every opportunity to remove water should be taken.

Creative placement of bars and steps in a complementary sequence prevents the bars from clogging with loose soil held in check by steps. Steps are in turn protected by waterbars that remove water from the trail and therefore keep the steps from washing out.

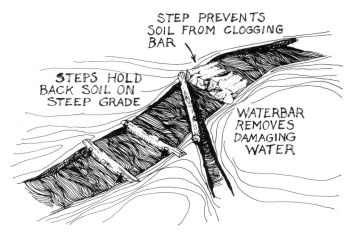

In steep-sided gullies where removal of water is difficult, steps may predominate. However, every possible exit for water should have a waterbar, even if it requires digging through the walls of the gully.

Installation — Once a site is chosen the first step is to dig a trench that will hold the waterbar. In order to divert the water efficiently, the waterbar and its trench must be at an angle. Generally the angle should be at 30 to 40 degrees to the treadway. Too shallow an angle will result in the water slowing down and backing up behind the waterbar; soil will eventually clog it in this place.

POOR ANGLE ON BAR HAS CAUSED SLOW WATER FLOW WHICH DEPOSITED SOIL AND LED TO EVENTUAL CLOGGING

The depth of the trench should be slightly greater than the diameter of the waterbar, enabling it once placed to be almost flush with the trail on its donwhill side. Too shallow a trench may leave the waterbar sticking up too high and increase the danger of water washing out underneath the log.

The length of the ditch should be at least as long as the log, and in most cases greater. On the lower end, to

CROSS-SECTION OF SOIL AROUND WATERBAR

ensure that the water is directed well off the trail, the trench is usually extended one to three feet beyond the end of the log unless natural topography adequately channels water away from the trail.

After the trench is dug and the log fitted into it, the waterbar can be staked securely in place. Hardwood or softwood saplings, two to three inches in diameter, can be cut into two to three feet lengths using a bow saw. One end is usually sharpened with an axe.

Three to five stakes can be used, one at the lower end of the waterbar and one or two on each side of it. Stakes on the uphill side of the bar should be notched into the log for added security and to minimize drag when water passes. When placing stakes, drive them in at an angle to form an inverted "V" over the log. This way the stakes fit tightly against the bar and actually hold the log down. Stakes should not stick up above the log, but should be driven or cut flush with the top of the waterbar.

STAKES

good   bad

A drawback with stakes is that after some wear and soil settling they may begin to stick up and form potentially hazardous projections to catch on pant cuffs and boots of hikers. Stakes may also get kicked out if hit repeatedly by hiker traffic. Keep them cut flush with the top of the log and placed near each end of it, out of the main flow of traffic. Or, a better solution might be to fit the bar into the terrain in a precise manner, minimizing the need for stakes.

Large rocks can also be placed on each end of a waterbar. This is preferable to stakes in that rocks are more aesthetic and permanent. Sometimes, with good planning and skillful use of tools, one can wedge a waterbar between existing boulders in the trail, eliminating the need for stakes.

USE ROCKS TO ANCHOR A WATERBAR WHEN THE SOIL IS TOO THIN TO TAKE A STAKE

Drainage Ditch — To optimize the positive characteristics of a well-placed waterbar, a drainage ditch should be used to collect water above the bar. If a trail is ditched on its uphill side, water traveling laterally through the soil will be caught in the ditch before it hits the tread of the trail. Then, after traversing the length of the ditch, it will be carried off by the waterbar.

In evaluating a trail section's drainage, use a ditch wherever necessary to develop permanent drainage pat-

DRAINAGE DITCH and BAR

terns that will leave the trail treadway hard and dry. With practice, trail workers develop a sense of what is required to drain and harden wet soils on trails on mountain slopes.

Drainage of a Switchback — If a switchback needs to be drained, one method is to direct water on the upper leg of the switchback to its upper side. Then the water, with the use of a ditch, can be properly and completely drained at the apex of the switchback, as illustrated below.

In some cases it may be necessary to drain water off the low side of the upper switchback. If this situation is encountered, a second waterbar on the lower leg of the switchback may be necessary to remove water completely, as shown in drawing No. 2.

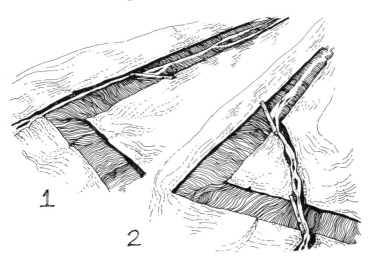

Final Steps of Installation — Once the waterbar is secure, pack soil up against its downhill side. On the uphill side pack some soil underneath the log to prevent water from undercutting it. A well-placed and properly secured bar can be almost maintenance free. During the life of a good bar it will channel water and deposit sediments in

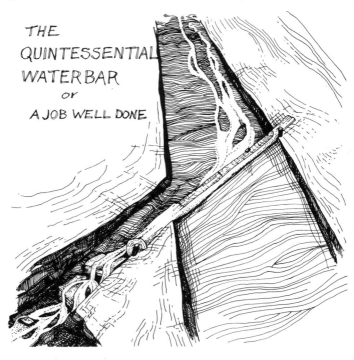

THE QUINTESSENTIAL WATERBAR
or
A JOB WELL DONE

such a way as to cause beneficial drainage patterns even after the wood of the waterbar has rotted and begun to deteriorate.

An important final step is to top the waterbar with an axe, making it rough-surfaced for good footing.

Waterbar Maintenance — Waterbars should be cleaned out annually in order to keep them working at maximum effectiveness. Deposited soil, leaf litter and organic matter will clog waterbars, especially those which are not self-maintaining. Debris should be dug out on the upper side, with sediments being spread over the trail below the bar. Any ditch that has filled in should be cleaned at the same time. A small, lightweight mattock is the best tool to use.

Rock Waterbars

These are not too commonly used, since suitable rock is generally not available. The principles of construction are basically the same as for a log waterbar.

Generally, flat and narrow rock is set into a narrow but deep trench. If the rocks are butted end to end tightly or overlapped in shingle fashion, water will not go between them. Placed solidly and properly, rock waterbars can provide a longer-lasting and more aesthetic alternative to peeled log waterbars. They are, for obvious reasons, more appropriate above treeline.

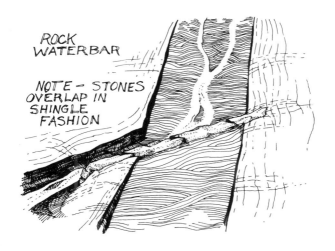

ROCK WATERBAR

NOTE — STONES OVERLAP IN SHINGLE FASHION

Drainage Dips — Drainage dips, often used on logging roads, are another water removal technique. Briefly, this technique involves digging a trench across the trail at an angle and making a fairly substantial mound (one to two feet high and equally thick) on the downhill side with the soil. Only if soils are quite stable is this effective; the mound can quickly break down from the forces of water and hiking traffic. Dips should be dug at a sharp angle (45-50°) to reduce the force of the flowing water and subsequent erosion against the mound. For added strength in the construction of drainage dips, logs or rocks can be laid under the mound as a foundation for the soil.

DRAINAGE
DIP —
CROSS
SECTION

Steps

Though probably less important in reconstruction than waterbars, steps grow in importance as trail slopes steepen. If a trail has moderate grades steps can be infrequently placed, and usually confined to just above the occasional waterbar, where they help prevent clogging. However, on steep ascents they are critical to soil retention and stabilization.

The basic purpose of steps is to provide a stable vertical rise on a trail while permitting lower average grades between steps. This slows water and retains soil.

Steps should be thoughtfully placed on the trail to ensure that hikers will use them. They have to be in the most attractive place to walk, usually a low place requiring the least effort on the part of the walker. This is an

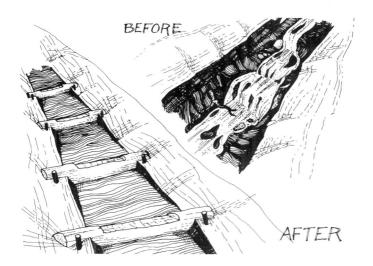

important point. Steps that rise too high above the surface of the ground will not be used by hikers. A new treadway will develop and hikers will create an eroded area immediately to the side of the unused steps.

Even steps that are well-placed are avoided by some hikers, particularly if they are tired and going uphill. It order to prevent this place dead wood or stones alongside the steps. Low and simple rock walls might be needed on heavily used trails or in alpine zones. The object is to make routes avoiding the steps unattractive or impassable, thus containing traffic on the stablized treadway.

Rock Steps — Rock steps are far more desirable than log steps, as they last longer and are much more aesthetically pleasing. One problem is that often there is not enough easily available rock with which to work. Rock steps are so far superior to log ones, however, that the additional effort required to obtain suitable rock is almost always justified. A persistent crew leader who searches out good rock is a valuable asset in these situations.

Any shape rock can be used; however, a large, flat-surfaced rock is much easier to work with and makes a more usable tread. As far as size goes, rocks used should probably weigh at least fifty to one hundred pounds. On seriously eroded trails much larger rocks have been placed with success. Smaller rocks are more apt to work loose eventually. The weight alone of a large rock will help keep it in place.

ROCK STEPS
CROSS-
SECTION

The basic tools needed to build rock steps are a crowbar, mattock and shovel.

In placing steps, either wood or rock, it is generally best to work up from the bottom of a slope. This procedure makes it easier to determine the best step placement and the best mix of stabilization techniques. When installing steps on very steep slopes, particularly rock steps, overlapping is sometimes necessary. This makes it imperative to work from the bottom up.

The first step is to find rock to be used, if possible uphill of the work and off the trail. Dig a hole in the trail to accommodate the rock and place it in the hole, presenting its flattest and widest surface as a treadway. Make sure the rock step is secure. It should not shift even slightly at any point on its surface when being used by hikers. This final part of the installation requires skill and patience. Many times rocks that are used are not large enough to provide a treadway of adequate width; thus, several must be put side by side. However, large, single pieces are preferable if they can be found.

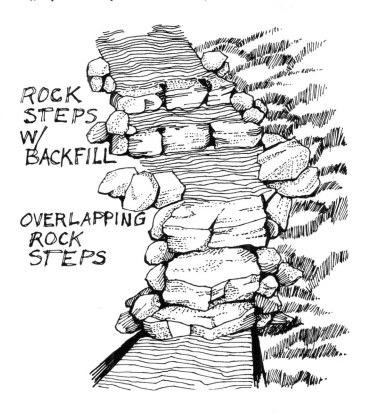

ROCK
STEPS
W/
BACKFILL

OVERLAPPING
ROCK
STEPS

When rock steps are put in on a steep slope, the rocks may need to be spaced closely, often overlapping lower steps by up to (or even more than) one-half their surface area. By overlapping large, flat rocks, each rock can add to the stability of the others.

Smaller rocks should not be used to "wedge" a step that is prone to rocking. They will eventually work loose. Each rock step should be solidly fitted in the soil and on other steps below. Large, solidly placed rock steps are the best technique for use on short, steep sections of eroded or eroding trail. They are often all that is available in alpine situations where erosion is occurring.

Rock steps may also be used to assist hikers up steep, ledgy areas which have been bypassed, causing damage to the steep soils to the sides of the ledge. By stacking large rocks on top of each other and by wedging them into any existing corners or cracks in the ledge, secure and attractive footing can be provided.

Care should be exercised in working with large rocks. Miscalculations when moving them can mean a crushed finger or worse. On steep slopes caution should be exercised to keep the rock from rolling past the work, endangering workers and hikers alike.

Wood Steps — The construction of wood steps is for the most part similar to building waterbars, except that steps are put in perpendicular to the trail and the uphill side of the log is backfilled and not trenched.

Spruce and fir are again the usual choices for wood; the diameter should be between six and twelve inches. On steeper slopes a larger diameter log gives more vertical rise. With small diameter stock, steps have to be very

LOG STEPS

NOTE — LARGER DIAMETER LOGS USED ON STEEP GRADE

close together and more numerous to provide the desired vertical rise.

The length of the wood steps depends on the width of the trail. When placed in a gully, the ends of the logs should extend into the banks. Too short a step will allow water and people to go around it.

The trench that the log is placed in should be roughly one-third the diameter of the log. The log is then set into the trench and secured with stakes similar to those described for waterbars.

Two stakes should be placed on the downhill side, one near each end, at an angle away from the log. Stakes should not be left protruding above the log, but should be driven or cut flush. If stakes cannot be driven, large rocks on each end will suffice.

Once the log step is secure, the uphill side can be backfilled with soil removed when digging the trench. When steps are placed in a series, ideally the bottom of the upper log should be just a bit higher than the top of the lower log, with the soil in between slightly sloped.

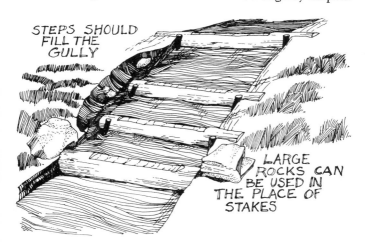

STEPS SHOULD
FILL THE
GULLY

LARGE
ROCKS CAN
BE USED IN
THE PLACE OF
STAKES

This will ensure a downhill slope and prevent puddling behind the step. As the rounded surface of the step can be slippery, the final touch is to slightly flatten the top of the log with an axe.

Special Techniques — In some cases where placing steps is not possible, more complex structures may be necessary. This usually occurs in very steep locations or along seriously gullied trails.

One such structure is what might be called a *combination ladder*, or a combination of cribbing and stepping. This technique is useful where a very steep slope or one with bedrock near the surface of the ground exists, making it difficult to secure regular steps.

It basically consists of building a log ladder and laying it into or up against the slope. Then each step is backfilled with gravel or rock scree. There should not be space behind the "rungs" which people might step into. Tops of the log "rungs" should be flattened with an axe.

There are many possible variations of this technique.

"CRIB LADDER"
RUNGS FIT INTO NOTCHES
AND ARE SPIKED
STEPS ARE BACKFILLED
WITH ROCK AND SCREE

Rock and Log Cribbing

Rock and *log cribbing* are techniques that involve creating a treadway on sections of trail that have severe gullying. In most cases the treadway is built on top of or along the side of the gully.

Steps can be put in a gully, but in a severely eroded area steps alone will not solve the problem of continued erosion. It may be more desirable to remove the trail from the bottom of the gully by using cribs.

Rock cribbing, which is the most aesthetic as well as the most durable, consists of using large rocks to strengthen the low side of the trail. On especially steep sidehill locations the treadway is actually constructed in rock wall fashion.

ROCK CRIB CROSS SECTION

A log crib consists basically of a log securely positioned alongside the edge of the gully. The log should be at least ten inches in diameter and peeled. Length depends on the area but generally a long, heavy log is best. The weight helps to hold it in place. It cannot be overemphasized that the log should be very secure, as it must support large amounts of soil and rock along with the weight of the passing hikers. It can be secured by large stakes or rocks, or butted up against rocks or trees. Logs perpendicular to the trail might be used as combination steps, spacers and retainers.

Cribbing techniques can also be used to shore up the banks above the trail treadway if it is steep and eroding.

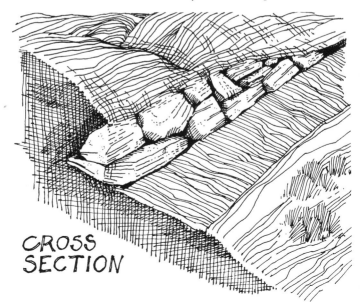

The uphill side of the tread can also be strengthened using log cribbing, which can be constructed in a number of ways, one of which is illustrated below.

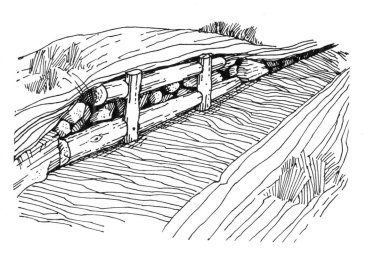

Retaining wall

Where the lower side of the trail is unstable, similar methods to those outlined above can be used. However, in constructing cribs or retainers for the lower side of the trail, one must keep in mind that the treadway should remain gently sloped to the outside or downhill side to ensure natural drainage. No crib or retainer should inhibit this drainage, nor should the treadway be flat or sloped toward the inside or uphill side of the treadway. Otherwise, water will puddle or flow along the tread.

The final step in cribbing is to fill in the gully with rock and wood debris to reduce further erosion and prevent hikers from traveling there. Ideally, the gully will begin to fill in again with forest litter and will recover.

8

HARDENING TRAILS IN WET AREAS

POPULAR TRAILS IN FLAT, LOW-LYING, WET terrain, as well as mountain bogs with highly organic, wet soils, are frequently plagued by destruction of plants and surface soil horizons. Wet, slippery, muddy locations develop very quickly on these soils, causing puddling of water on the trail treadway. Hikers, wanting to keep their feet dry, walk to the side of the tread and so cause a vicious circle of soil breakdown and trail widening. There are a number of techniques that can be applied to trails in this situation that will help to stabilize the damaged soils and allow trailside plantlife to recover.

Step stones, rock treadway or bog bridges made of native wood are the most frequently used solutions in these situations. However, before these techniques are used the drainage of the area under consideration should be investigated.

Wet, muddy locations frequently develop on trails because the treadway is lower than surrounding terrain.

Water draining laterally through soils becomes trapped on the lower surfaces that make up the treadway. Rather than bridge trails in these situations, a better long-term solution is to drain the wet area in question, especially if it is small and has a low end which, once ditched, would permit water to flow off the trail. Many times what looks at first glance to be a low, flat section of trail will actually have a very moderate slope and therefore an imperceptible flow of water. Small "flowing" wet spots such as this should be drained with waterbars and drainage ditches. The feasibility of this technique should be investigated before resorting to bridges.

If an area cannot be drained, or if for environmental reasons it should not be drained, and if relocation is not feasible, then trail hardening techniques should be used. These techniques offer dry passage for hikers and contain trampling damage on a hardened surface, thus allowing soils and plantlife to reestablish themselves.

Step Stones and Rock Treadway

If rock is available, it can be used to provide a longer-lasting and more aesthetic treadway than log bridges.

Step stones are basically just rocks set into the mud so that a stable and capacious treadway is formed. Any size

STEP STONE
TREAD
NOTE DRAINAGE
DITCH

Rock treadway can be used in place of bridge and, though more difficult to construct, it affords a more permanent solution.

and shape of rock can be used. Set them so the best surface walking upon is presented.

Step stones should be stable and must not protrude too high above the ground surface nor be so low as to be inundated with mud and water. Otherwise, people are apt to avoid them.

A *rock treadway* is simply a more intensive use of rock than is the case with step stones. Many rocks are set side by side, or are set into what is called a "rock box". With a *rock box*, a frame is constructed of logs which are peeled and spiked together, and rock is used to fill in the interior. With particularly good, square rock such a frame is not needed, since the rocks can be laid in flagstone fashion.

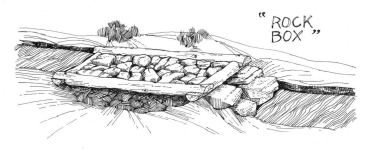

"ROCK BOX"

Bog Bridges

In areas where rock is scarce, which is often the case in boggy locations, log bridges can be constructed to form a hardened tread.

These bridges can also be used to ford small streams and gullies. In either case they will provide a dry, stable treadway. Life expectancy of such bridges is usually ten years or greater depending on species of tree, wetness of location and diameter and quality of wood used.

Basically there are two types of bridges, topped log and split log. Both are relatively simple to construct, re-

Log Bridge

quiring only a few hand tools. A third — but not often used — type consists of bridge stringers* made by sawing a log in half with a chainsaw. This produces a flat surface but involves a great deal of wear and tear on the chainsaw and the operator.

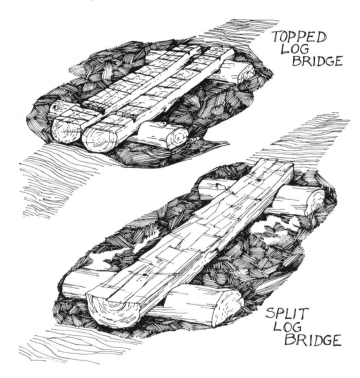

TOPPED LOG BRIDGE

SPLIT LOG BRIDGE

Topped log bridges are the most durable, and therefore the best bridges to use. Because the treadway logs are topped and have only approximately one-third of

---

Stringers are longitudinal parts of a bridge forming the treadway.

their mass removed, this bridge is stronger and more impervious to water, and therefore to rots than split log bridges. The stability gained from the extra weight of a topped log bridge is an added positive characteristic. Its major shortcoming is that it usually requires two full trees, which may make the split log bridge more feasible to install without running short of wood supplies on sparsely wooded boggy summits. The split log bridge, in addition to being economical with wood, is lighter and therefore easier to transport to its final location.

Topped Log Bridges — The only tool necessary in constructing a topped log bridge is a sharp axe; however, a chainsaw, if available, makes the work easier and faster. A peeler or bark spud greatly facilitates peeling, and a sledgehammer is good for driving spikes. Digging tools such as a mattock and shovel facilitate placing base logs.

As smaller diameter logs are used for stringers, usually two are needed side by side to provide a treadway of adequate width. Stringers should be no less than six inches in diameter; the average length should be around eight to ten feet. Both logs should be peeled to retard rot.

The base logs alone can be notched and the stringers set into them, or corresponding notches in both the stringers and base logs can be used. However, the stringers will be stronger if they are not notched.

Once the base log notches are cut, the two stringers can be placed on them. The space between the stringers should be no more than two to three inches, so that a foot cannot slip down between them. The stringers should be absolutely level.

Once the stringers are in place, a small notch roughly two inches square and two inches deep must be cut in the top of each stringer to accept the spikes. Spikes ten inches by three-eighths inch are recommended to nail the unit together.

SPIKE IN THROUGH
THE NOTCHES
STRINGERS
2-3" APART

After the stringers are spiked securely, the top of the stringers can be flattened. This can be done with an axe or an adz by hewing the upper surfaces; however, with a chainsaw it can be done more easily and quickly. Cuts are made with the chainsaw roughly every six inches and to a depth one-third of the way through the log. Then using an axe or an adz the top can be chipped off flat.

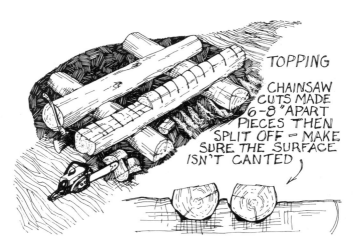

TOPPING

CHAINSAW
CUTS MADE
6-8" APART
PIECES THEN
SPLIT OFF — MAKE
SURE THE SURFACE
ISN'T CANTED

When topping the major thing to be careful about is that the bridge surface does not end up sloped to one side, a common problem with topped bridges.

PLACE BRIDGES NO MORE THAN 6" APART. ENDS OF STRINGERS SHOULDN'T TOUCH THE BANKS

Split Log Bridges — Split log bridges require the use of three tools primarily: a single-bit axe, an eight to ten pound sledgehammer, and four four to six pound steel splitting wedges. A peeler or bark spud, if available, greatly facilitates peeling, though an axe alone will do.

The diameter of a log to be split should be no less than ten inches. Length is up to the builder, but usually eight to ten foot stringers are used. Generally spruce or fir is used, since they are easy to cut, peel and split. They are also relatively lightweight, which aids when carrying them. Hardwoods split fairly well but are very heavy and hard to cut and peel.

In choosing trees to cut, look for ones that are the straightest and most uniform in diameter. Also look for trees with the fewest branches, which usually means fewer knots to contend with when splitting. Do not use trees with "heart rot."

Once the log to be split is felled, it must then be peeled. Though the peeled log can be a bit slippery to handle, the spiral of the grain and location of knots is then visible. Also, during the splitting process the split can easily be seen and corrected should it begin to angle off to one side.

The next step is to look over the log and choose a line of split. If there are many knots, try to pick a line that will go between them if possible. The splitting process itself is begun by driving the axe into the center of one end. It is often easiest and best to begin at the larger diameter end. This initial end split will provide a good, straight starting split from which you can work, lengthening it until the log is split in half.

Next, drive a wedge into the top of the log in line with and near the starting split. As you drive in the wedge the split will lengthen. Drive the wedge in until only the top two to three inches are showing, or until the split begins to spiral off to one side.

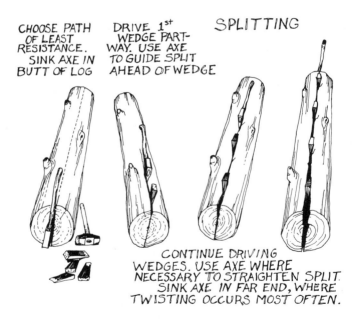

CHOOSE PATH OF LEAST RESISTANCE. SINK AXE IN BUTT OF LOG

DRIVE 1st WEDGE PARTWAY. USE AXE TO GUIDE SPLIT AHEAD OF WEDGE

SPLITTING

CONTINUE DRIVING WEDGES. USE AXE WHERE NECESSARY TO STRAIGHTEN SPLIT. SINK AXE IN FAR END, WHERE TWISTING OCCURS MOST OFTEN.

If spiraling occurs, take the axe and carefully make several chops to bring the split back in line, then drive the wedge in further. Be careful not to hit the axe handle or your knuckles on the wedge.

Continue to alternately drive wedges and chop in between them until you reach the end of the log. If four wedges are not enough, leave the first one in place and remove the middle ones, driving them in leapfrog fashion beyond the last one. As you near the end, drive the axe into the butt to ensure a straight end split.

The log should now be almost completely split in half, held together by a few resistant strands on the bottom side. Remove two wedges and leave two in, one near each end; then roll the log over. Using the two wedges and your axe, carefully finish the split. Be careful not to let the stringers splinter where they are held by resistant strands or they may be weakened or left with a twist. Cut off any large loose splinters.

The next step is to cut two base logs for each stringer. Again, spruce and fir are probably the best choice. The diameter should be at least ten inches and the length at

NOTCHING
NOTE - 2 POINTS OF CONTACT
ON SIDES OF STRINGER

HERE, THERE IS A
GAP TO ONE SIDE.
THIS WILL ROCK.

least three feet. In cases where a muddy area is very deep or wide, a longer base log may be desirable to keep the bridge from tilting or sinking.

Notching is the next step. A single U-shaped notch in the base log into which the stringer fits is strongest. Corresponding notches in the base log and stringer can be axed out and the two fitted together; however, this will weaken the stringer.

ANGLE THE SPIKES IN OPPOSITE DIRECTIONS

No matter which method is used, once the base log is stable, the stringer seated and the treadway surface level, the whole unit can be spiked together. Spikes ten inches by three-eighths inch are recommended.

When spiking, one trick which helps make a more stable bridge is to angle the spikes slightly in opposite directions. This reduces the likelihood of rocking. After the bridge is spiked together, look at the surface of the stringer. If it has a ridge in one spot or is twisted, use the axe to flatten it out. Do not hit the spike!

Bridge Construction Reminders — Whether you build a split log or topped log bridge, in order for it to be effective it must be used by the hiker. Make sure that the treadway width is sufficient to make walking on it easy. In some cases it may be necessary to use double stringers, two side by side — or in the case of particularly thin stock, three in parallel.

The treadway should not be tilted or angled to one side, nor should the bridge be unstable, rocking or very springy. With stringers that are over eight to ten feet long or are very springy, use three or more base logs for support. It is probably best to keep bridges short and therefore stable.

The height of the bridge surface should not be over eight to ten inches from the ground. A high bridge is hard to step up onto or off of, and can be difficult to traverse for those averse to heights. Trench in the base logs if the unit will be too high or if it will otherwise rock.

Also, a rocky or dry, stable soil should be found at the end of a bridge, not mud or slippery roots. When bridges are placed end to end, a space of no more than six inches should separate them.

Caution should be exercised when bridging on pond shores or in any areas that are prone to flooding in wet seasons. If water levels rise substantially, bridges will float and drift off the trail. This might happen, for instance, along a pond shore that has beaver activity. Trails in these situations might best be relocated rather than bridged.

9

TOOLS: USE, CARE AND SUPPLIERS

THE PURPOSE OF THIS CHAPTER IS three-fold: to generally acquaint the trail maintainer with various types of tools and equipment; to briefly outline their proper use, care and applicable safety procedures; and, to provide information on sources where such tools can be purchased.

The types of tools used in trail maintenance will vary depending upon the type of work engaged in. One should always have the right tool for the right job. Following are descriptions of basic tool types and their applications.

In addition to describing hand tools, this chapter will discuss some basic power tools. However, information provided on their use is limited; the manufacturers of this equipment can supply a great deal of information that will adequately meet the requirements of any owner.

Experience has taught that only top quality tools should be purchased. To make use of "bargain" tools will usually only result in headaches for the trail worker.

Cutting Tools

Cutting tools are the most important type used in trail work. All trails require clearing of trees and brush during their initial development, as well as annually thereafter.

Cutting tools are also the most difficult and elaborate tools in terms of the maintenance they require and the difficulty that the maintainer will have in procuring them. All hardware stores carry simple cutting tools such as axes, saws and pruners; however, these are more often than not made of poor quality steel.

Tools covered here include axes, saws, pruners, machetes and specialized tools such as brush or bush hooks and safety axes.

The Axe — The axe is undoubtedly one of man's oldest tools. It has played a tremendously important role throughout history. In America it has probably played a more important part than the rifle in the country's development. It was in America that the axe reached its highest form; nowhere else in the world has it been used so much, undergone so many changes and seen so many adaptions to different uses. Unfortunately, today the axe is diminishing in its importance and popularity. Because of this it is very difficult to find a good axe made with high quality steel.

The axe, however, continues to be an important tool in clearing and maintaining trails. On the AMC trail crew it is the primary tool used to cut logs for trail reconstruction. It is also important in keeping trails clear.

If used correctly and maintained properly, the axe can be just as effective, efficient and safe as the crosscut saw or even (in the case of long distance backcountry trail work) the chainsaw. It is lighter than the chainsaw and does not require as many accessories. In addition to being a very practical tool for trail work, it is also a very aesthetic tool which, because of its ancient roots, has great appeal for many trail workers. Aside from replacing the handle every year or so, maintaining an axe is an expense-free proposition, unlike the continued cost of operating a chainsaw.

The two basic kinds of axes are the single bit and the double bit.

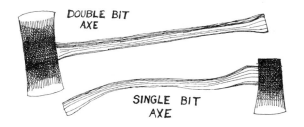

DOUBLE BIT AXE

SINGLE BIT AXE

Both are used for removing blowdowns, limbing, felling trees, cutting notches and waterbars, and topping bridges.

The single bit is the more familiar of the two types. The double bit was more popular in the past, when axemen needed to have two blades, one that was kept extremely sharp for felling, limbing and notching and the other for chopping close to the ground or in situations which would otherwise dull the good edge. The double bit also has a better balance for dropping trees. The cutting edge is balanced by the duller edge at the other end of the blade.

For safety reasons a single bit has gained in popularity. The butt of the single bit axe can also be helpful for occasionally pounding stakes. However, care should be used in this situation, because the axe head can quite easily be beaten out of shape and the eye become too wide for the wooden handle. It is best to use a sledge-hammer for operations which require heavy pounding.

The axe is a very personal tool. The type of axe as well as the style of the head is usually a matter of taste on the part of the axeman; however, the job that the axe is going to be used for is also an important criterion. Single bit axes are the easiest to find, and therefore will probably be the best choice for most people.

The size of the axe is one personal aspect of choosing a good tool. Normally chopping work should be done with a three to $3\frac{1}{2}$ pound axe head. Smaller people may prefer a lighter axe. Big folks might want a four or even $4\frac{1}{2}$ pound axe; however, they should probably try one out before selecting this larger size. In addition to the weight of the head, the length of the handle is an important consideration. Shorter people want a shorter axe handle, whereas taller people want a longer one. If the axe is going to be used for clearing small brush and working in cramped quarters, then a smaller handle is more appropriate.

A good quality axe is made of two different kinds of steel. Mild steel, which is softer and therefore more resistant to impact, makes up the eye or the body of the axe. The edge of the axe is made of a harder carbon steel that is forged to the body; it will take and hold a sharp edge. Most axes that are available on the open market are drop-forged and made of one kind of steel. Because of this they are usually hard and brittle, making it difficult to maintain a good edge. They are also somewhat more prone to metal fatigue. Some of these drop-forged axes have even broken when they have been used on frozen or hard wood. In shopping for an axe look for a seam and hammer marks between the eye and the edge of the axe; this indicates that it is made of two different kinds of steel. An axe head that is painted or otherwise obscured, especially in the vicinity of the edge, is probably drop-forged. A good place to look for a good quality axe is at an antique store or antique sales. The older axes found in such circumstances are often handmade and of a much higher quality than modern mass-produced axes.

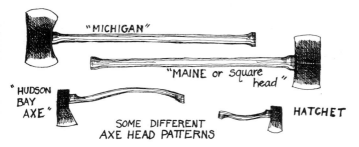

"MICHIGAN"

"MAINE or square head"

"HUDSON BAY AXE"

HATCHET

SOME DIFFERENT
AXE HEAD PATTERNS

Sharpening an Axe — All cutting tools, including axes, are actually safest when kept sharp. This is because the axe will penetrate the wood rather than deflect in a dangerous glancing blow. It is the dull tool that can deflect out of control. Besides being safer, sharp tools are obviously much more efficient to use.

Sharpening an axe well can be tedious; however, it is a fairly straightforward process, requiring only time, practice and a few simple implements. The most critical aspect of the axe edge is the *bevel*, which is basically the shape of the edge itself.

USE A LOW SPEED
WHEEL AND KEEP
IT **WET**
ALSO NOTE ANGLE
OF AXE TO
WHEEL

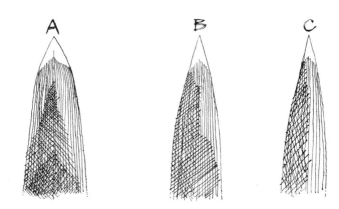

Bevel A usually develops in an older axe that has been improperly maintained. Sharpening has obviously been concentrated on the edge, which in turn has rounded out the steel into a fairly blunt profile. Bevel B is the proper bevel. The axe is thin enough so that it penetrates deeply into wood but not so thin, as in Bevel C, as to make the edge fragile and prone to breaking. To work a bevel down and get it into shape, as in B above, work the steel down with either a good manual stone on a wheel or a flat bastard file. When using a wheel, always keep its surface wet to carry away any grit that would clog it up, as well as to prevent friction and overheating of the axe head.

Never use an electric grinding wheel to sharpen an axe, as the heat will destroy the temper of the steel. If a hand or foot powered wheel is not available, a flat bastard file can be used. Always sharpen into the blade; otherwise, the edge will become a small piece of wire-like metal that will break off with use. By sharpening into the blade, this burr will not form. One should use extreme care when sharpening in this manner, because the hand is proceeding in the direction of the blade. It may be best in this situation to wear a good pair of heavy leather gloves.

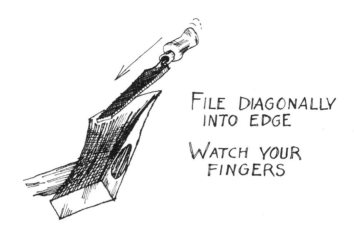

FILE DIAGONALLY INTO EDGE

WATCH YOUR FINGERS

Work the bevel down until it looks thin enough to slide easily into wood behind the cutting edge. Once the proper bevel is attained, take a round handstone and hone the edge smooth. If a very keen edge is desired, a finer stone such as an Arkansas handstone can be used. This final part of the process can produce an edge that is fine enough to shave with.

START GRINDING FROM 3" BACK AND WORK TOWARD EDGE

A FAN SHAPE WILL REINFORCE THE CORNERS

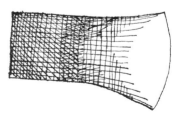

Again, it should be emphasized that an axe should be kept as sharp as possible at all times. Maintaining a "keen edge" is well worth the effort.

Rehandling an Axe — Handles wear out and require eventual replacement. Sometimes they warp or get cracked or broken — or the head may loosen, in which case the axeman will want to replace the handle.

The first step is removal of the old handle. The easiest and fastest way to do this is to saw the handle off the axe head. Then place the head in either a vice or on wooden blocks and drill out the wood in the eye of the axe with an electric or hand-operated drill. By boring out these holes, the pressure of the wood within the axe head is relieved so that the wood can be removed with a hammer and a blunt metal object.

Choose the new handle considering the desired length. A 32-inch handle is appropriate for most people and most situations. When purchasing a new handle look closely at the grain of the wood. It should be fairly straight and close together. If the grain is wide or is not parallel with the axis of the handle, it is probably weak and prone to breaking. Avoid knots at all costs.

Hickory or ash are the best woods for handles because they have a lot of spring and strength. Avoid handles which are painted, since painting covers up any faults in the wood.

The next step involves fitting the handle into the eye. Use a draw shave, wood rasp or spoke shave to shape the eye down to the size of the head. Remove wood cautiously so that you do not make the handle too thin. Once you can get the head to slide one-third of the distance onto the axe handle, you have probably shaved off enough wood. If the handle head has not been cut down the center at the factory to accept a wooden wedge, you will have to cut a slit yourself. Place the handle in a vise and cut it carefully with a carpenter saw, keeping it centered.

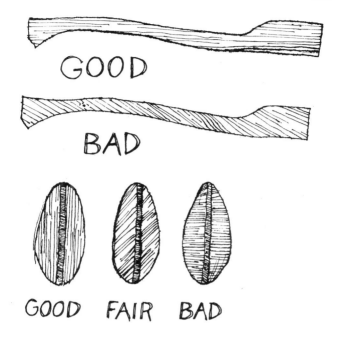

GOOD

BAD

GOOD   FAIR   BAD

PAY CLOSE ATTENTION TO
THE END GRAIN— A TIGHT
GRAIN PARALLEL TO THE
WEDGE IS BEST

Cut it about two-thirds as deep as the eye of the axe head
is long.

At this point the handle can be held vertically so that
the head is down and a hammer used to pound it into
the eye of the axe. Pound the handle in so that it goes
past the top of the axe head and comes down to the
proper place on the handle. At this point the excess

wood sticking out of the top of the axe should be cut off and a hardwood wedge driven into the axe head to secure it in place. Using a wooden wedge is better than using a metal one because metal crushes the grain of the wood within the eye of the head, this weakens the axe and makes it prone to loosening.

DRIVE HANDLE INTO HEAD WITH A WOODEN OR LEATHER MALLET

Care of the Handle — There are several improvements the axeman can make on his handle which will make it easier on his hands. Proper care can also eliminate dry rot, loosening and premature cracking of the handle.

Store bought handles come with either a paint or a hard spar varnish finish which, with extensive use, can cause blistered hands. A finish of boiled linseed oil is best. Apply it with a brush or rag after sanding off the store-bought finish.

To extend the life of a handle, linseed oil can be periodically placed in one or two holes drilled in the end of the handle; the holes should be one-quarter inch in diameter and one-half inch deep. At the end of the work day, place several drops of linseed oil in the holes and set the axe upright to soak overnight. The natural capillary action of the wood will draw the oil into the grain.

FEED YOUR AXE

PUT LINSEED OIL IN THE HOLES DRILLED IN THE HANDLE — ADDS LIFE!

If a handle loosens within the head of the axe, a temporary solution is to soak the axe head in a bucket of water overnight. This causes the wood to swell and tighten within the head. Mind you, this is a temporary solution. The handle should eventually be replaced.

This is a very cursory overview of taking care of an axe. Patience and presistence will help the axeman gain the skills necessary to care for his tool.

Axe Sheaths — All axes should be sheathed, to protect both the edge of the axe and people when the axe is being transported or stored. There are many different kinds which can be purchased or made by the axeman. The most common ones on the market are leather sheaths with snaps.

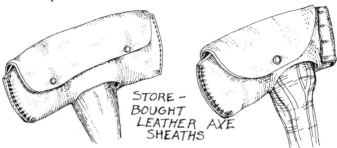

STORE-
BOUGHT
LEATHER AXE
SHEATHS

Simple sheaths can be made using rubber from an old garden hose. The hose is cut to the width of the blade and slit along its length. This piece is held against the edge of the axe with a piece of rubber inner tube. This method can also be used with a hollowed out block of

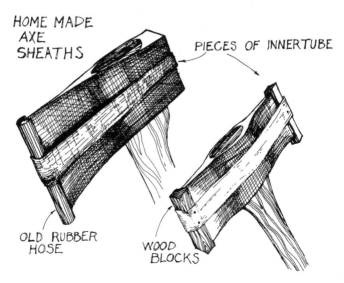

HOME MADE
AXE
SHEATHS

PIECES OF INNERTUBE

OLD RUBBER
HOSE

WOOD
BLOCKS

wood instead of hose. Wood is obviously more secure and stronger than rubber hose. Wood is also less prone to slipping off the blade.

The Swizzle Stick — This important and versatile tool was developed for clearing brush and low growth along hiking trails. Similar tools are commercially available; however, they lack the strength and durability of the homemade variety.

The swizzle stick is used in a swinging motion similar to a golf club, except that the double edge enables the worker to cut on the backswing as well. The swizzle should always be used in a conscientious fashion, with two hands on the handle to fully control the swing. A rock or stump may accidentally deflect the tool; therefore, always wear heavy boots when using this tool and maintain a good distance between trail workers.

A sheath should be used when carrying and storing the swizzle. A strip of heavy canvas wrapped around the blade and held in place by inner tube rubber shaped in a figure eight is the best method. Adhesive tape can be used in a pinch, though.

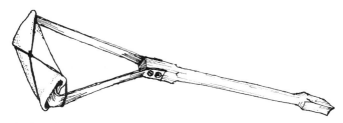

Swizzle Stick

Sharpening — A round stone should be used to sharpen the cutting edges. Should the edges get very dull or battered from use, a flat mill bastard file is a helpful preliminary to the stone. Sharpen only on the low side of the blade; otherwise, sharpening is similar to that used on the axe.

Construction of the Swizzle Stick — Construction of the tool is quite simple. A hardwood handle is used, with ash or hickory preferred. In a pinch a sledgehammer handle will do. Someone with a wood lathe should have no problem making one. The steel frame can be easily bent using a torch or forge. The blade is the most difficult part, requiring the help of a machinist or blacksmith to get the proper temper to hold a good cutting edge. The edge should not be too hard or it will break upon striking a rock or root, but is cannot be too soft either or it will not hold an edge.

In putting the swizzle together the bolts holding the blade to the frame should be heat treated for strength. Flat washers are necessary in order to dissipate vibrations from impact. Without them the blade will soon begin to fatigue and crack. When using the tool in the field it is a good idea to carry spare bolts, nuts, washers and wrenches. To minimize loosening and loss of bolts and nuts, the end of the bolt can be hammered or filed, or the commercial compound Locktite can be used. The bolt can also be drilled with a hole and a cotter pin inserted.

Customizing a swizzle stick involves lengthening or shortening the handle. Some maintainers wrap black electrician's tape around the handle, sometimes with a thin piece of foam or ensolite, to cushion the handle slightly. A large knot on the end, either shaped from the wood or from wrapping it with tape, helps keep the hands from slipping off.

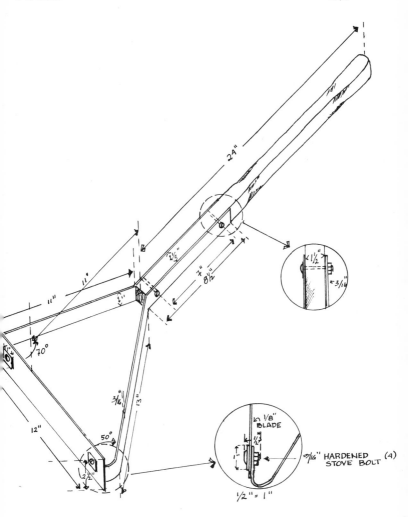

24"

1½"

7"

8½"

11"

11"

1"

70°

12"

3/16"

13"

50°

2½"

‹1½"

‹3/16

⌐ 1/8"
BLADE

9/16" HARDENED (4)
STOVE BOLT

½" = 1"

Plan for swizzle

The frame can also be changed, shortening or lengthening one side or the other, to get a sharper angle. Some prefer to have the blade horizontal to the ground when holding the tool out at the angle they are most comfortable with.

Safety Axe, Bush Hook and Machete — These can be handy supplements to the more classic tools used for trail clearing. They require care and sharpening similar to that described for the axe.

The safety axe recommended is Swedish. This tool is good for younger, less experienced trail workers because the blade is less exposed than that of an axe or machete. If the blade is damaged, it can be replaced. It is particularly effective on young, springy hardwood growth.

SAFETY AXE

The bush or brush hook is another type of tool available for clearing brush.

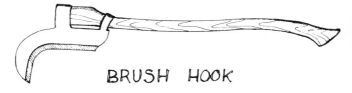

BRUSH HOOK

The best machete is the Woodsmen's Pal. It has some features, such as a cutting hook, which are unavailable on a conventional machete. It is also shorter than the conventional tool, which allows a shorter, more controlled swing. Generally, this tool is unnecessary, since the pruner cuts the same size brush in a neater and safer manner.

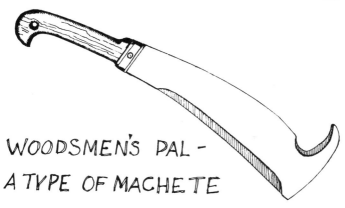

WOODSMEN'S PAL - A TYPE OF MACHETE

As with the swizzle stick, all of these tools should be used with care. A good grip at all times, plenty of space between workers, and a little looking and thought before swinging will prevent accidents and damage to the tools.

With the Woodsmen's Pal in particular, if the hook is used in pruning limbs or cutting or uprooting under-growth, caution must be exercised. Many people grab the limb or bush with one hand to toss it away once it is cut. They hook it at the base and pull toward them. If the hook slips it may catch the fingers of the other hand. In swinging the Woodsmen's Pal be careful not to bring it too near your head. You might catch your shirt collar, ear or the side of your head with the hook.

The sharpening of all these tools can be done with a round stone and flat bastard file. All should have store-bought or homemade sheaths, as outlined above for the axe.

Lopping shears, pole clippers and hand pruners — Long-handled clippers, pruners or lopping shears come in a variety of styles. Handles are made of wood, steel or aluminum. Cutting heads are either the sliding-blade-and-hook type or the anvil type. Some have simple pivot actions, while others have compound or gear-driven ac-

DIFFERENT TYPES OF PRUNERS

SLIDING BLADE TYPE WOODEN HANDLES

ANVIL TYPE w/ WOODEN HANDLES

COMPOUND GEAR DRIVEN TYPE

RACHET TYPE

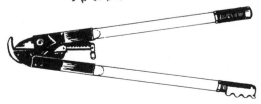

tions for increased cutting power. Most cut between one and 1¾ inch limbs.

For specialized work such as clearing ski touring trails, a variety of pole clippers are manufactured for professional tree trimming work. These are suitable for clipping high limbs up to one or 1½ inches in diameter. Generally a six to eight foot handle is sufficient for ski touring trail work.

Pole Clippers

Small hand pruners can sometimes be quite handy for occasional light pruning. These also come in a wide variety of styles.

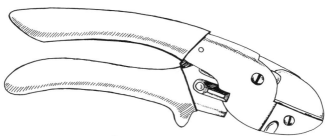

SMALL HAND PRUNERS CAN SOMETIMES BE QUITE HANDY FOR OCCASIONAL LIGHT PRUNING. THESE ALSO COME IN A WIDE VARIETY OF STYLES

As clippers or lopping shears are one of the primary tools of the trail maintainer, it is important that high quality ones be obtained. Look for brand name shears that are built for rugged use and that are simple to maintain and repair. Some of the cheaper models available have handles that are simply glued or riveted on loosely. The blades are made of steel that is too soft. Some can be bent by cutting small hardwood bushes or limbs. Also, some poorly made ones of the sliding blade type are flimsy or the stops do not meet correctly. When pressure is applied and the stops slip by each other, the handles come together and pinched fingers result. Head assemblies and gear mechanisms should be tight, not loose with lots of play in them.

The compound gear clippers are very ruggedly built for heavy duty cutting; however, they tend to be a bit on the heavy side. Experience suggests that the gear driven clippers with the anvil type blade and the wooden handled sliding blade type of clippers are superior.

Clippers should be kept sharp and all metal parts lightly oiled. A flat file or handstone works well for sharpening the blade. In the sliding blade type of pruners, only the outside edge of the cutting blade should be sharpened.

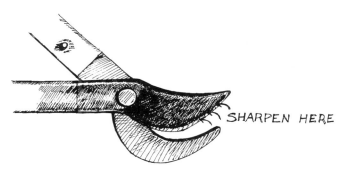

SHARPEN HERE

By concentrating sharpening on the curved outside edge of the cutting blade, the jaws of the pruner are forced together during the cut. Sharpening the inside edge of the blade will form a bevel that will tend to force the jaws apart during the cut. The anvil-type pruners are sharpened on both sides of the cutting blade.

Crosscut Saws — There are two types of crosscut saws.[6] The one-man crosscut, three to 4½ feet in length, is designed to be used by one man on small timber; however, it can be converted into a two-man saw if desired by attaching a supplementary handle at the end of the blade. The two-man crosscut, generally five to eight feet in length, is designed for cutting larger diameter timber.

[6]Most of the information on crosscut saws was developed using *Crosscut Saws: Description, Sharpening, Reconditioning*, U.S. Department of Agriculture, Forest Service, Equipment and Development Center, Missoula, Montana, April, 1974.

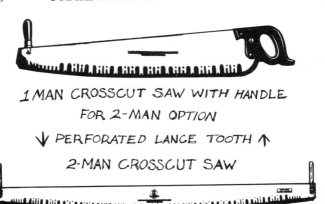

1 MAN CROSSCUT SAW WITH HANDLE
FOR 2-MAN OPTION

↓ PERFORATED LANCE TOOTH ↑

2-MAN CROSSCUT SAW

Three common tooth patterns are available, each designed for a specific type of wood. The perforated lance tooth style is best for cutting softwoods. The champion tooth style is for cutting hardwoods or frozen timber. The plain tooth style is designed for cutting dead, dry wood.

PERFORATED LANCE TOOTH

CHAMPION TOOTH

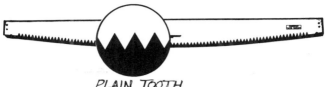

PLAIN TOOTH

In trail work a crosscut is rarely used. The axe is fa-vored for most cutting, with the chainsaw being used for special large-scale projects and the bow saw for small sawing needs. As is the case with the axe, the crosscut has become for the most part a tool of the past because of the development of the mechanized chainsaw.

CUTTING ACTION OF CROSSCUT SAW

How the Teeth Cut — The cutting teeth sever the fibers on each side of the cut. The raker teeth, cutting like a plane bit, peel the cut fibers and collect them in the gullets between the cutting teeth and raker teeth and carry them out of the cut. A properly sharpened cross-cut saw cuts deep and makes thick shavings.

Crosscuts do, however, have some advantages over the axe and even the chainsaw which may make them a good choice for large cutting projects. They are inexpensive, lightweight, non-polluting in terms of noise and air, safer than the axe, and relatively easy to use and maintain. If used and cared for properly, they can be just as efficient and effective as the chainsaw, especially when the tool must be carried long distances. Sometimes, however, finding someone who can sharpen a crosscut properly can be a problem. If this proves to be the case, small, relatively inexpensive sharpening kits can be obtained by the trail maintainer.

As for use and safety tips, a few things should be kept in mind. When felling timber you should use the same basic technique as outlined for felling with a chainsaw or axe. To keep your crosscut from binding, carry a small container of kerosene and lightly coat the blade with it. For transporting a crosscut, the best sheath is one made of two strips of plywood held together over the blade with three or four bolts.

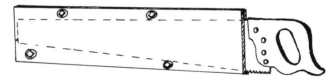

PLYWOOD SAW SHEATH

Bow Saws and Pruning Saws — Bow saws, sometimes known as pulpwood saws, and the smaller pruning saws come in a wide variety of sizes and shapes with a corresponding variety of uses. The choice of saw depends on the type and amount of work to be done.

The larger bow saws are best suited for cutting small diameter timber and are used for tasks such as removing blowdowns and clearing limbs and saplings. Some of the larger, older bow saws have wooden frames. Today most such tools have painted or chrome-plated steel or aluminum frames and blades ranging in length from 24 to 36 inches.

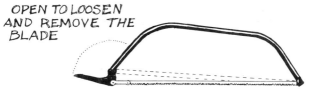

OPEN TO LOOSEN
AND REMOVE THE
BLADE

BOW SAW WITH DISPOSABLE BLADE
AND CLAMP-TYPE HANDLE

The smaller pruning or utility saws used the most in trail work are good for sawing small diameter timber such as stakes for log steps and waterbars. They are also good when clearing trail where saplings or limbs are too large for clippers and it is undesirable to leave a pointed stump, as sometimes happens when using an axe or brush hook. There are some collapsible saws on the market which are handy for the occasional user; however, they are generally too lightweight for continuous, heavy-duty use.

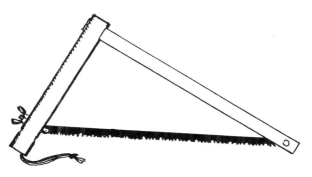

COLLAPSIBLE SAW
FOR BACKPACKING

A GOOD SMALL
PRUNING SAW

For light hand pruning there are a number of good folding pruning saws on the market. For specialized work there are various manufacturers of professional tree trimming equipment who have hand pruning saws. Some have teflon-coated blades for ease of action. There are also various types of pole saws which can be used for cutting high limbs when clearing ski touring trails. Both of these types of saws have teeth that cut on the pull stroke only.

Use and care of these saws is quite similar. Almost all of the bow saws and pruning saws have blades which are replaced rather than sharpened, whereas the professional pruning saws and pole saws can be sharpened. Saw sharpening is an elaborate skill; usually specialists (frequently "old timers") can be found on a local basis. See "Further Reading" and equipment suppliers for further information.

When using these saws, be sure that all moving parts such as nuts and bolts are secure, with the blade at the right tension if it is adjustable. If it is too loose or too tight you will end up with a broken blade when it flexes or gets pinched in the wood. Trail experience points toward preference for those saws with the smallest number of movable or adjustable parts (such as wing nuts), which invariably get lost. It is also wise to bring spare

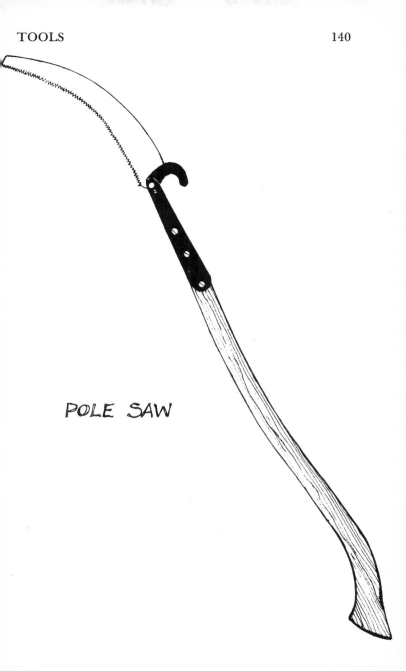

POLE SAW

blades and parts when working in the field so that minor repairs can be made.

When transporting or storing saws, some type of sheath should be used to protect the worker as well as the blade. Wood, leather or heavy canvas can be used. Many bow saws come with hard plastic sheaths. All metal parts should be kept lightly oiled when not in use to prevent rust.

Digging Tools

Virtually all trail reconstruction activities require that workers move soil to build steps, waterbars, drainage ditches, bridges and similar projects. Digging tools for accomplishing these tasks are the shovel, mattock, pick and crowbar.

These tools are very common and no instructions on their use need be given here. There are several types of each, however, that serve specific purposes.

Shovel — This tool comes in two forms, the long handle and the "D" handle.

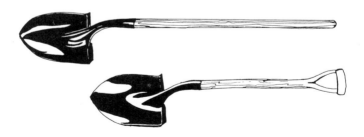

Long handle and "D" handle shovels

The long handle is generally more appropriate in digging deep holes, whereas the "D" handle, being shorter, is more appropriate in congested situations. Care should be used not to pry too heavily with the shovel; otherwise, the handle will break. The mattock or crowbar should be used if large rocks impede digging.

Mattock — In the White Mountains the mattock has become the most important digging tool because of the large quantities of rocks in the mountain soils there. The mattock is a heavy tool that is not easily broken. When used vigorously to dig through roots and to pry and sometimes break rock, surprising amounts of work can be done.

There are two types of mattocks available, both of which have an adz, or a blade set at right angles to the handle; each features a pick or a cutter blade.

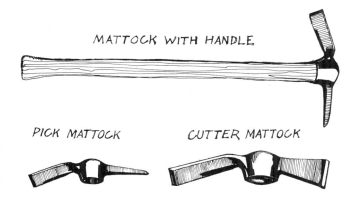

MATTOCK WITH HANDLE

PICK MATTOCK   CUTTER MATTOCK

The pick mattock is more popular with AMC crews because it is much more effective for prying the rock characteristic in White Mountain work. The cutter mattock may be more effective in areas with deeper soils and more roots than rocks.

Care consists of periodic sharpening in order to maintain a rudimentary edge capable of effective digging. An electric grinding wheel, though hot on the steel, reduces labor time when sharpening. Handles need periodic replacement, so an adequate stock should be kept on hand.

Pick — A pick is rarely necessary in trail work, its function being adequately served by the pick mattock. However, in jobs which involve a lot of rock work, picks may be appropriate.

Crowbar — This tool is an essential one for moving large rocks. With practice the crowbar can become surprisingly effective as a lever for moving great weight. The trick is to place a fulcrum with care and forethought. In order to be most effective the crowbar should have a wedge-shaped tip. Avoid pointed tips.

Crowbar

Measuring Tools

Various tools for measuring distances may be required during layout, reconstruction and maintenance of trails. Levels, transits and a theodolite may be necessary in unusually fine map work in laying out a trail or campsite; however, if this degree of accuracy is needed, it is probably best achieved by hiring professionals.

Measuring wheels are used to measure trail distances for guidebook descriptions. They can also be used for marking off an index system for record keeping and work assignments for crews. The rugged, all-steel measuring wheel, with the counter mechanism contained inside rather than outside where it may get snagged on brush and damaged, is probably the best type to use.

Power Tools

Though the bulk of trail work involves the use of hand tools, there are occasions where concentrations of

Measuring wheel

heavy cutting or specialized work make power tools more efficient. Information on the chainsaw, motorized brush cutter and jackhammer are included here. Because manufacturers have much good information on the use and care of these implements, only a broad description of the tool and its specifications are given here.

Chainsaws — The chainsaw comes in an extensive variety of makes, sizes and types, each of which is suited to a particular job. Each of the major manufacturers of chainsaws carry a full line of equipment that graduates in size and power from small six to eight pound saws to the large machines used by the pulp and paper industry.

Choosing a make and manufacturer is a matter of personal choice, like choosing an automobile, and the range of opinions among users is as great as the selection itself. The choice of make might most appropriately be determined by investigating what dealerships are available in the purchaser's area. Having a good dealer who provides prompt and efficient service is probably more important than the characteristics of the saws themselves, particularly if the final choice is between any of the large manufacturers that specialize in chainsaws. Chainsaws manufactured by the large department store outlets are best avoided.

The smaller saws available from each of the major manufacturers are naturally the most popular saws for trail work because of their light weight. Larger, more powerful saws are more appropriate for particularly heavy cutting such as would be the case with major storm damage or when it is necessary to clean up a trail damaged by timber harvesting. These situations are fairly rare for most maintainers, however.

Features to look for in shopping for a saw, after one has decided on an appropriate size, include the general "feel" and appearance of the saw, and the accessibility of controls and components — particularly the spark plug, which needs periodic replacement, and the gas and oil filler caps which, if on the same side of the saw, eliminate the need to rotate the unit during fill-ups. All saws should have a throttle-lock which allows the operator to free his hand from the throttle in order to start the saw safely with both hands — one hand to hold the saw on the ground and one to pull the cord.

Most modern saws have a safety feature on the handle which prevents the engine from revving up unless the operator has a firm grip on the saw. Another feature to look for is whether hand grips are rubber mounted to reduce the effect of tiring vibration on the hands. The effectiveness as well as the position of the muffler should also receive consideration. The newer saws are surprisingly quiet and if the muffler is on the front of the saw or on its right side directed away from the operator, then noise and exhaust fumes are less of a problem. The chain needs to be oiled as it rotates on the guidebar; therefore, saws are equipped with either manual or automatic oilers. The automatic is perferable if it is dependable, because while the operator is concentrating on a cut he may neglect to oil his chain, which increases bar and chain wear.

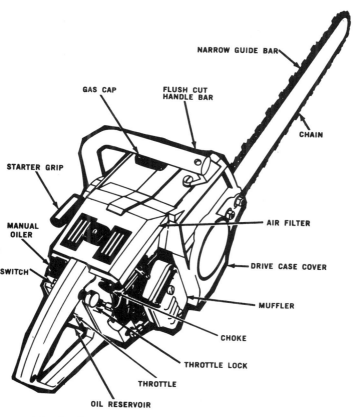

A drawing of a typical chain saw with the various exterior parts labeled.[7]

[7]Drawing from Bromley, W. S., *Pulpwood Production,* Interstate Printers and Publishers Inc., Danville, Illinois, 1969, p. 122. The text following relies heavily on the same source.

This cursory overview is provided to help people select and purchase saws. The manufacturers supply extensive information which the discreet shopper will do well to read. The opinions of friends and fellow maintainers are also an obvious — and dependable — source of good information on the comparative value of different saws. It may also be beneficial to talk to either a professional tree trimming outfit or a logging operator working in the purchaser's local area. The types of saws they use and their recommendations on dealerships may be helpful.

Safe Chainsaw Operation — Safe chainsaw operating techniques should be constantly stressed to all power tool users. The chain operates at a fast cutting speed and the slightest slip or miscalculation can bring extremely serious injury.

There are protective devices available for chainsaw operators and they should be used. They include helmets, eye protection and, for particularly loud saws used on a long-term basis, ear protection. Additionally, leather gloves should be worn, as well as heavy leather boots with non-slip soles, preferably equipped with steel toe shields. Loose fitting, long-sleeved shirts and long pants are warranted.

CHECK LIST
FOR THE SAFE AND EFFICIENT OPERATION
OF YOUR CHAINSAW

☐ READ YOUR OWNER'S MANUAL AND ALL SUPPLEMENTS (if any are enclosed) thoroughly before operating your saw.

☐ DON'T USE ANY OTHER FUEL than that recommended in your Owner's Manual.

☐ REFUEL IN A SAFE PLACE. Don't spill fuel or start saw where you fuel it. Do not refuel a hot saw; allow it to cool off. Be certain the saw has dried thoroughly before starting if fuel has spilled on the unit.

☐ DON'T SMOKE while fueling or operating the saw.

☐ START YOUR SAW WITHOUT HELP. Don't start a saw on your leg or knee. Never operate a chainsaw when you are fatigued.

☐ KEEP ALL PARTS of your body and clothing away from the saw chain when starting or running the engine. Before you start the engine, make sure the saw chain is not contacting anything.

☐ BEWARE OF KICKBACK! Hold saw firmly with both hands when engine is running; use a firm grip with thumbs and fingers encircling the chainsaw handles and watch carefully what you cut. Kickback (saw jumps or jerks up or backward) can be caused by —

— Striking limbs or other objects accidentally with the tip of the saw while the chain is moving.

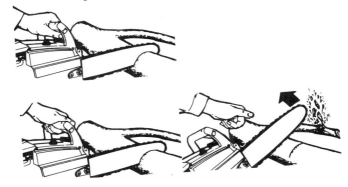

Using a chainsaw

In the upper lefthand corner, the correct way for holding the upper grip of a chainsaw is shown, with the thumb under the grip. The two lower illustrations show what can happen when the thumb is placed on top of the grip.[8]

---

[8]Bromley, p. 130.

— Striking metal, cement or other hard material near the wood, or buried in the wood.
— Running engine slowly at start of or during cut.
— Dull or loose chain.
— Cutting above shoulder height.
— Inattention in holding or guiding saw while cutting.

☐ IT IS STRONGLY RECOMMENDED that you do not attempt to operate the saw while IN A TREE, ON A LADDER or ON ANY OTHER UNSTABLE SURFACE. If you elect to do so, be advised that these positions are EXTREMELY DANGEROUS.

☐ BE SURE OF YOUR FOOTING and pre-plan a safe exit from a falling tree or limbs.

☐ WHEN CUTTING A LIMB THAT IS UNDER TENSION be alert for springback so that you will not be struck when the tension is released.

☐ USE EXTREME CAUTION when cutting small size brush and saplings because slender material may catch the saw chain and be whipped toward you or pull you off balance.

☐ VIBRATION — Avoid prolonged operation of your chainsaw and rest periodically, especially if your hand or arm starts to have a loss of feeling, swell or become difficult to move.

☐ EXHAUST FUMES — Do not operate your chainsaw in confined or poorly ventilated areas.

☐ OBSERVE ALL LOCAL FIRE PREVENTION REGULATIONS — It is recommended that you keep a fire extinguisher and shovel close at hand whenever you cut in areas where dry grass, leaves or other flammable materials are present.

NOTE: Spark arrester screens are available for installation in your muffler, where fire regulations require them. Check local regulations for your special requirement.

☐ TURN OFF YOUR SAW WHEN MOVING BE-
TWEEN CUTS and before setting it down. Always
carry the chainsaw with the engine stopped, the
guide bar and saw chain in the rear, and the muffler
away from your body.

☐ USE WEDGES TO HELP CONTROL FELLING
and prevent binding the bar and chain in the cut.

☐ DON'T TOUCH or try to stop a moving chain
with your hand.

☐ DON'T ALLOW ANY OTHER PERSON OR
ANIMAL CLOSE to a running saw or where a tree
is being cut down.

☐ DON'T TOUCH or let your hand come in contact
with a hot muffler, spark arrester or spark plug wire.
Don't run the saw without a muffler, exhaust stack
or spark arrester. Keep screens and baffles clean.
Keep spark plug caps clean and in good repair. Replace promptly if necessary.

☐ KEEP THE CHAIN SHARP and snug on the guide
bar.

☐ DON'T ALLOW DIRT, FUEL, OR SAWDUST
to build up on the engine or outside of the saw.

☐ KEEP ALL SCREWS AND FASTENERS TIGHT.
Never operate a chainsaw that is damaged, improperly adjusted or not completely and securely assem-
bled. Be sure that the saw chain stops moving when
the throttle control trigger is released. Keep the
handles dry, clean and free of oil or fuel mixture.

Jackhammers — The various applications of the self-
contained, gas-powered jackhammers were discussed ear-
lier; therefore, only technical features will be outlined
here.

These tools are powered by a single cylinder, two-cycle
engine which provides power for three basic operations:
(1) movement of an impact piston which provides the
impact on the drill bit, (2) rotation of the drill bit, and
(3) compression of gas and transmission through the drill
bit which blows dust out of the hole.

These self-contained units can be packed into remote locations by two crew members; one of whom carries fuel and all accessories. Such units are considerably more limited in their power and applications than is a conventional jackhammer, which is operated by a large and powerful compressor on a trailer or the back of a truck; however, it does enable maintainers with trail problems involving rock to solve them.

There are two manufacturers, both in Sweden. Literature on the features of their equipment will be provided to persons making inquiries.

Pionjar Distributors   Cobra Distributors
Abema, Inc.   Atlas Copco.
129 Glover Ave.   70 Demarest Dr.
P.O. Box 775   P.O. Box 312
Norwalk, CT 06856   Wayne, NJ 07470

Drill bits, shims and wedges can be purchased from Bicknell Manufacturing Company, Rockland, Maine.

Gas-Powered Brush Cutters — These power tools can be beneficial for heavy trail clearing through young, heavy growth such as can be found after an area has grown back following logging. Most maintainers will not have a need to invest in this specialized piece of equipment. It is acknowledged here to let readers know that the tool exists and can be used for certain trail situations.

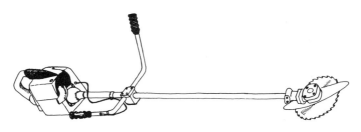

Gas-powered brush cutter

Other Tools

Bark spuds or peelers can greatly facilitate peeling logs for trail construction. Before the modern, automated de-barkers used at sawmills and paper mills were invented, all bark removal was done by hand using these simple but effective tools.

Bark Spud

Come-alongs or cable jacks are sometimes needed for moving large rocks or logs. Most are available with varying pull capacities, anywhere from one ton to three or four tons. The lighter, open-faced, ratchet type with cable is most commonly used. Cable, chain or tire chains can be used to wrap a rock for moving it.

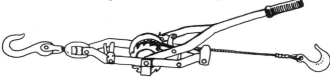

Cable Jack

Splitting wedges or woodchopper's wedges, most commonly used to split firewood, are also used to split logs for split log bog bridges. Weights and sizes vary, but generally a four to five pound one, eight to ten inches long and 2½ to three inches wide is best.

Splitting wedge

Packboard — The Appalachian Mountain Club has developed a packboard to use in resupplying their hut system, and for use by trail crews going out into the field for a week at a time. It is much more rugged and heavy-duty than any packboards available on the market. Its main purpose is for carrying heavy loads (80-120 pounds) over relatively short distances (3-5 miles). It is included here for those maintainers planning heavy-duty reconstruction work.

The frame is made primarily out of straight-grained white ash, a strong and resilient wood that can withstand the stresses and strains of heavy loads.

The following is a listing of the other materials needed, along with where they can be purchased.

1. Page Belting Company, 26 Commercial St., Concord, NH 03301 (603-225-5523):
    a) Oak leather pieces for tote harness — 26" long x 2½" wide, 9-10/64" thick, oil dressed.
    b) 1" copper rivets with burrs, 6-10 gauge (sub ⅞").
2. Any hardware store:
    a) No. 414 nickel buckle with imitation roller, 1¼" — manufactured by Covert Manufacturing Company, Troy, NY.
    b) No. 514 ¼" x 2½" Alt No. 4R2 eye bolt and nut — manufactured by Hindley Manufacturing Company.
3. Fortune Canvas, 190 US Rt. 1, Falmouth, ME 04105 (207-781-2628):
    a) pack corset.

The approximate cost of all materials should run around $40.00.

Safety Equipment

Besides the various sheaths used to protect blades and users, there is a variety of safety equipment available.

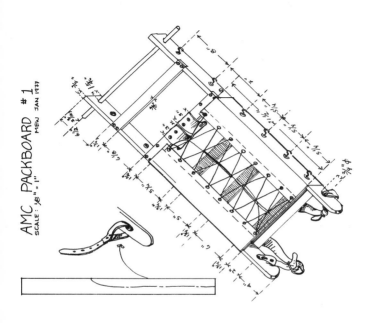

AMC PACKBOARD #1
SCALE: 1/8" = 1"
MEW JAN 1977

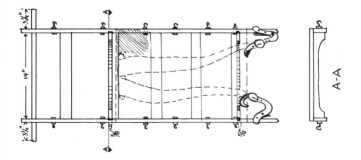

A-A

Hardhats come in many styles, colors and materials. Strong, good quality and comfortable hats should be selected. Color, though seemingly insignificant, can make a difference, in that white or aluminum colored ones are much cooler than dark ones on hot summer days.

Steel-toed boots are recommended for chainsaw work. Also available are chaps or leggings and chest pads made of very strong but lightweight mesh, much like a bullet-proof vest, to give the chainsaw user some margin of protection from cuts.

Safety goggles or face masks are appropriate in chainsaw work and when using a brush cutter or jackhammer. Heavy protectors are also available and should be used when operating motorized tools. Ear protection should be worn if extensive cutting is planned.

Shin guards used by baseball catchers are sometimes used by maintainers engaged in extensive digging with mattocks. Leather work gloves are preferred by some to protect hands from blistering and cuts.

SUPPLIERS OF TOOLS, EQUIPMENT AND MATERIALS FOR TRAIL WORK

In order to facilitate the maintainer's ability to find tools for trail work, the following list of suppliers has been compiled. This list is not complete; it will, however, enable the trail worker to search out the major suppliers meeting his equipment needs. Many of the more common tools, of course, can be purchased from hardware stores, department stores and the like. The suppliers listed as wholesale will send you a catalog and refer you to dealers in your area. They will not sell directly to you.[9]

---

[9]A portion of this material was developed using tool listings supplied by the U.S. Forest Service, Equipment Development Center, Missoula, Montana 59801.

Measuring wheel

TABLE 1

Tool	Numbers correspond to companies listed in Table 2
Axe, Hatchet	2, 3, 4, 6, 10, 15, 17, 24, 32, 33, 34, 38, 41
Bark Spud	32, 38, 41
Brush Hook, Bush Hook	2, 4, 6, 14, 17, 21, 34
Bow Saw	2, 4, 5, 6, 13, 17, 27, 31, 33, 39, 40, 41
Come Along, Winch	6, 17, 29, 39, 40
Crowbar, Mattock, Pick Hoe	5, 6, 22, 35, 36
Crosscut Saw, Handle	4, 6, 17, 20, 27, 33, 38, 41
Crosscut Saw Sharpening Kit	9, 41
Clipper, Pruner, Lopping Shear	1, 2, 4, 6, 7, 11, 13, 17, 18, 19, 31
Flagging Tape	6, 17
Handles for Axe, Sledge, Mattock	5, 25, 30, 32
Lay-out Equipment (Compass, Inclinometer)	6, 17
Machete, Woodmen's Pal	4, 6, 10, 11, 17, 26
Measuring Wheel	6, 8, 17, 28
Mini-Mattock (for waterbar maintenance)	3, 24
Pole Pruner, Pole Saw	1, 2, 4, 6, 13, 16, 17, 19, 23, 31, 37
Pruning Saw	2, 4, 6, 12, 13, 16, 17, 23, 27, 31, 34, 37
Pulaski	4, 6, 10, 17, 32
Safety Equipment	6, 17, 37
Sheath	5, 6, 17, 32, 37
Splitting Wedge	4, 6, 17, 24, 32, 35, 36
Swedish Brush Axe	4, 6, 17
Swizzle, Weeder, Scythe	2, 6, 11, 14, 21

TABLE 2

1. American Standard Co., 1 West St., Plantsville, CT 06479
2. Ames, Div. of McDonough Co., PO Box 1774, Parkersburg, WV 26101(W)
3. Army Surplus Stores, most cities
4. Bartlett Mfg. Co., 3003 East Grand Blvd., Detroit, MI 48202

5. Belknap, Inc., "Bluegrass", PO Box 28, Louisville, KY 40201 (W)
6. Ben Meadows Co., Forestry & Engineering Supplies, PO Box 8377, Station F, Altanta, GA 30306
7. Brookstone Co., "Hard to Find Tools", Peterborough, NH 03458
8. Cedarholm Mfg. Co., Bastrop, TX 78602
9. Century Tool Co. Inc., Ginko Industrial Park, 102 Richard Rd., Ivyland, PA 18974
10. Collins Axe, PO Box 351, Lewiston, PA 17044 (W)
11. Columbia Cutlery Co., PO Box 123, Reading, PA 19603
12. The Cooper Group, PO Box 728, Apex, NC 27502
13. Corona Clipper Co., PO Box 730, Corona, CA 91720
14. Council Tool Co. Inc., PO Box 165, Lake Waccamaw, NC 28450 (W)
15. Estwing Mfg. Co., Reading, PA 19603 (W)
16. Fanno Saw Works, PO Box 628, Chico, CA 95926
17. Forestry Suppliers, Inc., Box 8397, Jackson, MS 39204
18. G. F. Hickock, 2344 Stanwell Cir., Concord, CA 94520
19. H. K. Porter, Inc., 74 Foley St., Somerville, MA 02143 (W)
20. Jemco Tool Corp., 60 State St., Seneca Falls, NY 13148
21. John Houchins and Sons Co., 400 W. Market St., Newark, NJ 07107 (W)
22. Leetonia Tool Co., 142 Main St., Leetonia, OH 44431
23. Fred Marvin & Associates, Inc., 1968 Englewood Ave., Akron, OH 44312
24. Marion Tool Corp., Marion, IN 46952
25. New England Handles, PO Box 187, Thompson, CT 06277
26. Oley Tooling Inc., Oley, PA 19547
27. Pennsylvania Saw Corp., 810 Broad St., Newark, NJ 07102 (W)
28. Rolatape Corp., 1301 Olympic Blvd., Santa Monica, CA 90404 (W)

29. Sanal Industrial Inc., Concord, NH 03301
30. Sequatachie Handle Works Inc., Sequatachie, TN 37374
31. Seymour Smith & Sons, Snap-cut Garden Cutting Tools, Oakville, CT 06779
32. Snow & Nealley Co., 8494 Exchange St., Bangor, ME 04401
33. Stanley Tools, Div. of Stanley Works, New Britain, CT 06050 (W)
34. True Temper Corp., 1623 Euclid Ave., Cleveland, OH 44115 (W)
35. The War Wood Tool Co., Wheeling, WV 26003
36. The Warren Group, Div. of Warren Tool Corp., Hiran, OH 44234 (W)
37. W. M. Bashlin Co., Grove City, PA 16127
38. Woodcraft Supply Corp., 313 Montvale Ave., Woburn, MA 01801
39. Sears and Roebuck
40. Montgomery Ward & Co.
41. Antique Stores

(W) = Wholesale

Packboards in use

FURTHER READING

Trail Construction

1. *Trail Manual for the Appalachian Trail*, 6th edition, 1966, $1.00 PP. Appalachian Trail Conference, Box 326, Harpers Ferry, W VA 25425.

   A manual giving good instructions on layout, cutting and blazing.

2. *Trails Manual*, Charles Vogel, price unknown. Equestrian Trails, Inc., 10723 Riverside Dr., No Hollywood, CA 91602.

   A manual oriented to western horse trails. Good presentation of basic drainage requirements.

3. *Forest Service Trails Handbook* (FSH 7709.12). U.S. Forest Service. (They are hard to get. Try to visit the Forest Service personally if you want a copy.)

RAWFORD PATH

OLDEST CONTINUOUSLY—USED
MOUNTAIN TRAIL IN AMERICA

Crawford and his son, Ethan Allen, cleared this
e near the top of Mt. Clinton. Along this trail
guided many groups to the summit of Mt.
e trail was improved to a bridle path in 1840
75 years old, making the first ascent of Mt.
horseback. By 1870 this historic path
original use as a footpath to the heights.
sands have traveled this path to the Presid—
d Mt. Washington.

WHITE MOUNTAIN *National Forest*

Pretty good rundown of some construction techniques. Again, western oriented.

4. *Trail Planning and Layout*, $3.00. Audubon Society, Nature Center Planning Division, 950 3rd Avenue, New York, NY 10022.

    Very good on construction and layout of nature trails and other trailside interpretive facilities.

5. *Trail Construction Manual*, price unknown. Tennessee Department of Conservation, 2611 West End Ave., Nashville, TN 37203.

6. *Pacific Crest Trail*, 1971, price unkown. U. S. Department of Agriculture, Forest Service, 14th St. and Jefferson Dr., SW Washington, DC 20250.

7. *Guide to Vermont Ski Area Trail Construction and Management*, Pamphlet No. 39 price unkown. Agricultural Experiment Station, University of Vermont, Burlington, VT 05401.

8. *The Nature and Properties of Soils*, 7th edition, price unknown Macmillan Company, Harry O. Buckman, Nyle C. Brady.

Landowner Liabilities

9. *Incentives to Use of Land for Outdoor Recreation Purposes: Insulation from Tort Liability; Tax Relief*, University of Georgia Law School. Bureau of Outdoor Recreation, Southeast Regional Office, 148 Cain St., Atlanta, Georgia.

    A good rundown on the legal liability of landowners who open the lands for recreational uses such as hiking.

State Trail Reports

10. *Report of the Rhode Island Trail Advisory Committee*, 1974, free. Rhode Island Statewide Planning Program, 265 Melrose St., Providence, RI 03907.

    This report discusses opportunities and current problems confronting the Department in the establishment of a trail program and recommends actions to correct these problems.

11. *New Hampshire Statewide Trails Study*, 1974, price unknown. State Office of Comprehensive Planning, State House Annex, Concord, NH 03301.

    This report contains the findings and recomendations of a year-long study of the potential for a State-wide Trails System for New Hampshire.

12. *North Carolina Trails Committee Annual Report*, 1974, price unknown. Department of Natural and Economic Resources, Raleigh, NC.

    This first annual report presents a summary of the North Carolina Trails Committee's work and findings for calendar year 1974.

Ski Touring

13. *The Ski Tourer's Manual*, 1975, price unknown. Ski Touring Council, Troy, VT 05868.

Off-Road Vehicles

14. *The Off-Road Vehicle and Environmental Quality*, Malcolm F. Baldwin and Dan H. Stoddard, Jr., 1973, $4.00. Conservation Foundation, 1717 Massachusetts Ave., NW, Washington, DC 20036.

    An updated report on the social and environmental effects of off-road vehicles, particularly snowmobiles, with suggested policies for their control.

15. *Trails: A Strategy for Snowmobile Fun and Safety,* 1975, price unknown. Snowmobile Safety and Certification Committee, Inc., 1755 Jefferson Davis Highway, Arlington, VA 22202.

   This draft version has been prepared exclusively for review by governmental officials and other members of the snowmobile community, and as a means to generate further discussion in the important area of winter outdoor recreation facilities.

Tools

16. *Crosscut Saws: Description, Sharpening, Reconditioning,* price unknown. U.S. Department of Agriculture, Forest Service, Equipment and Development Center, Missoula, Montana.

Hewing a bridge stringer

APPENDIX

TRAIL DESIGN ON PRIVATE LAND

Introduction

ABOUT TWO-THIRDS OF ALL HIKING IN THE United States takes place on state, county and private land.[1] Of this, private land will be the most important area for future trail development. Crowded public properties will soon reach a saturation point that will require corresponding development of hiking trails in the private sector if opportunities for hiking are going to keep pace with growing demands.

This trail development on private land is a great challenge because in addition to the requirements for satisfactory hiking and the design considerations relative to soils, topography and vegetation, the designer must satisfy the demanding and varied requirements that landowners will make conditional to use of their properties.

---

[1]Lucas, Robert C. and Rinehart, Robert P., "The Neglected Hiker", *Backpacker 13*.

Trail development on privately-owned local property provides recreational opportunities near home. Town and county parks become more available to the general citizenry if access is enhanced with trail development, and residents gain recreational opportunities normally reserved for vacation times and places removed from their day-to-day community environment.

Environmental education can be an important trail function, especially at the local level where the school curriculum can be developed to take advantage of nature study that is available with local trail development.

In addition to the obvious recreational value of trails on private land, there are many conservation and land use values which may follow from a successful trail installation. Trails connecting conservation districts add continuity to public protection efforts. Trails, by channeling people sensitive to environmental quality through the landscape, help to protect land by building a protection-oriented constituency. The environmental considerations of trail design require, by their very nature, the documentation, cataloging and use of lands having high natural amenity. Exercises in trail layout in the private sector are exercises in continuous connection of open space property.

This appendix on trail design on private property describes the different kinds of landowners and their general concerns with trail use on their property. Techniques for determining ownership and for negotiating with owners are outlined. This information is presented with the idea that the organization sponsoring the trail is trying to secure a legally binding right-of-way from owners in order to guarantee protection of the trail environment in the future.

Determining Ownerships in a Proposed Trail Corridor

After an initial documentation of trail needs is done and a decision is made to proceed, investigation of ownerships should then be carried out. In order to maintain flexibility that will be needed in negotiating with owners, a broad trail corridor including alternate trail locations should be outlined during the initial stages of planning.

Following is an outline for researching landowners[2]:

1. Obtain access to town tax maps if they exist. If so, they are usually kept by the Assessor's Office or the Town Clerk. The maps always public information and are available for anyone to examine. The information is quite complete, although the boundary lines are not always accurate and do not claim to be so. However, they are close enough for this stage of the project. The owner's names, addresses and acreage are given, and any easements over the property should be marked.

2. Research deeds in the county Registry of Deeds. In addition to checking names and addresses, it is important to look for any easements or restrictions which might already apply to the property. If the town has no tax maps, the process is far more complex, a bit like doing a jigsaw puzzle. Following are some suggested methods:

   a) Ask local residents, generally those who are sympathetic to the trail project, for general landownership patterns, specific owners if known, and ideas on who would be most favorably inclined toward

---

[2]Kittredge, Lucia, in an unpublished work on the Monadnock-Sunapee Greenway Project, sponsored by the Society for the Protection of New Hampshire Forests, Concord, NH, 1974.

the idea of a trail and land preservation. Find out who else would know landowners and, if necessary, ask for an introduction. Local residents are probably the most useful sources of information because they are familiar with the use of land over time, attitudes toward conservatioon, financial status of individual owners and future plans for the region.

b) Talk to town Selectmen. If supportive of the idea, they are a good source, often knowing from memory who owns what land. The Selectmen's Office should have complete lists of property owners within the town, together with acreage, addresses and taxes paid. (However, they may have no maps showing boundaries.) They also can give an idea of how much land is being sold in the town, what the various land uses are and what future plans might affect the trail. It is a good idea to maintain a good working relationship with the town Selectmen, as they may be useful when actually talking with landowners.

c) Talk with surveyors who have surveyed land in the area. Often a few surveyors have been working in a region for a number of years and know the land and landowners well, particularly with regard to the larger landholdings. They are a good source of information on existing woods roads, current use of the land and outstanding natural features, and their familiarity with landowners makes them a likely contact when landowners are approached.

d) Conservation officers of state Fish and Game Departments, county foresters and consultants from the Soil Conservation Service are another source of information. Often they know a particular area well and can recommend certain landowners who would be more favorably inclined to the project than others. Their greatest help, however, is in knowing the land and its features.

e) The chairperson of town Conservation Commissions are extremely helpful in most cases, especially as they are sensitive to the conservation attitudes prevalent in the town. Again, they can be most useful when actually contacting landowners.

Types and Patterns of Ownership

The types and patterns of ownership play an important role in the design and layout of a trail. Studying overall types and patterns of landownership helps to describe the path of least resistance, and therefore the easiest and most economical direction for the trail to follow.

1. **Corporate Owners — Pulp and Paper Companies, Agricultural Ownerships** — Lands held by corporations for timber harvesting and agriculture can be ideal for trail use. Well-planned trail use can be easily adapted to the management programs of these ownerships. The typically large size of forest ownerships lessen the degree of negotiation required of the trail designer per unit of trail mileage gained.

These lands are not disrupted by trail use in the same way residential land would be, being agricultural in nature. Hikers are less aggravating to absentee owners than they are to residential owners who confront the use directly.

Corporate owners make virtually all management decisions on the basis of the financial benefits that accrue to the company's shareholders. Their posture is predictable and consistent; they demonstrate the preeminent practicality of the business establishment. In this light, they are leery of any legal encumbrances that might follow a successful and popular trail installation.

In order to successfully approach these owners with a trail proposal, the designer must have prepared management plans acknowledging their concerns. These concerns generally are oriented around how the trail will foreclose future owner options. Enthusiastic use by the public would make closure a bad public relations issue; accidents could pose an unacceptable liability burden on the owner; and, the very real concerns of fire hazard, parking congestion, vandalism and sanitation problems can make endorsement of trail proposals by these owners difficult.

2. **Corporate Owners — Developers and Subdividers —** Owners whose purpose is to develop their landholdings are almost always decidedly negative toward proposals for trail use. From their viewpoint, trails unrealistically foreclose their options.

Development land virtually precludes the possibility of high-quality trail design because of its usually piecemeal character and its tendency to be subdivided into small units. There have been many cases where existing trails were closed because access had been cutoff by development. Many informal, unmaintained paths around cities and towns have been effectively closed in recent years by urban sprawl: limited access highways, airports and the like. Development land sadly but effectively narrows trail options and the possibility of success for public trail use.

3. **Residential Owners —** In towns and near urban centers, most ownerships are residential — i.e., owners live on or close to their property. These ownerships require closer, more thorough follow-up for trail installation. Owner attitudes are more varied and therefore the design, in order to meet these varied perspectives, becomes more complex.

A conservation-minded owner will be easier to negiotiate with because he shares and can understand the social and environmental goals of the proposed trail. Work, therefore, will be facilitated if owner attitudes are documented in the initial research where possible. This way, when the negotiation stage is reached, the most sympathetic owners can be approached first. Endorsement from these owners will help their less sympathetic neighbors to accept the idea of public trail use. Protection of trails on residential land, depending on the situation, can be so complex as to be unrealistic for trail projects over the long term.

Concerns of Private Landowners

Owner concerns with public trail development, more particularly with any accompanying legally binding arrangement proposed for the property in question, are legitimate. Try to see a trail proposal from the owner's perspective.

1. **Future Use of the Proposed Trail Property** — The major concern evident in negotiation for protected trail rights-of-way is that of the landowners for maintaining their future options for use of property proposed for the trail. Trails need not be protected with legal agreements; however, without some protection the trail's future cannot be securely guaranteed. Therefore, the negotiator should propose that some minimum distance around the trail be kept free of incompatible developments such as structures and timber harvesting activity. This distance could be anything from eight feet to a quarter of a mile depending on the owner, the financial resources of the trail sponsor and the value of the proposed trail. Care should be used in negotiating to anticipate the owner's reaction so that the proposal does not sound unreasonable. The sponsor must temper his negotiations with sound judgments on the owner's attitudes. In initial transactions, it may be best to simply secure a written pledge from the owner to continue to work with the trail sponsor toward installation and eventual protection.

Legal agreements that protect trails, because of their linear nature, easily bisect owner's property into compartments which can place a serious constraint on its use, particularly for smaller owners. The right-of-way agreement should permit motorized crossing of the corridor plus limited use of vehicles along the trail treadway. This concession, plus the latitude to cut timber according to a simple prescription, offers the possibility of some protection to the trail while giving the owner the freedom he feels is essential in the management of his lands.

The legally binding agreement may require a commitment too great for the owner to accept. The small owner's desire to adapt his land program to changing conditions in his personal or family life or, in the case of corporate owners, the need for latitude to make decisions based on market changes are highly valued and constitutionally guaranteed freedoms.

If this degree of protection is not possible on a trail route for which no alternatives exist then the agreement should be adapted to the owner's conditions. In many cases the owner's plans preclude trail development altogether. If this is the case then not too much can be done to change the situation. Alternative routes must be found.

Of course, a policy of requesting less commitment from owners makes installation easier. In some cases the best course of action may be to simply get verbal or, better, written permission from the owner. This may be the best approach with reticent owners. After careful installation and high-caliber maintenance work geared to winning the owner's support, a gradual program of increasing protective efforts may be more feasible. The practice of the past, of just getting verbal permission for trail use, will diminish in importance in the future. The tenuous status of most trails on private land must be fortified with viable agreements to protect and perpetuate these facilities. If they are not protected, development will further reduce satisfactory hiking opportunities in the future.

2. **Landowner Concerns — Liability for Hiker Injury —**
A second major concern owners frequently have is
that they would, by giving approval to the proposed
trail, be tacitly accepting an unreasonable degree of
liability for accidents that hikers may have on their
property.

Inherent in our whole concept of private land is
the owner's right to control his land. Because of this
control posture the courts have historically held that
the owner can prevent hazardous conditions or give
warning of hazardous conditions to users of his land.
Failures to provide this protection of visitors could
be construed by the courts as negligence, which would
be the first step in any legal proceedings against a
landowner by an injured hiker.

Proving negligence on the part of a landowner requires four elements:[3]

1. Duty or obligation recognized by law requires the
   owner to conform to a certain standard of conduct for the protection of others against unreasonable risk.

2. The failure on the owner's part to conform to the
   standard required.

3. A reasonably close causal connection between the
   conduct and the resulting injury (proximate
   cause).

4. Actual loss or damage resulting to the hiker's interest.

3. **Extent of Duty — The Legal Obligation of the
   Owner —** Identification of the extent of duty is im-

---

[3]Harrington, Robert F., "Liability Exposure in Operation of
Recreation Facilities", *Outdoor Recreation Action*, No. 35,
Spring, 1975, pp. 22-25.

portant because, as indicated in the outline of requirements for negligence, liability is predicated upon one's breach of duty owed to another.[4] This extent of duty owed by an owner to users of his land depends upon the legal status of the person using that land. The legal status of users of land can be divided into three broad categories: (1) trespassers, (2) licensees, and (3) invitees.

The duty of landowners is different for each of these three categories. This sliding scale of legal obligation increases as the status of the visitor increases from trespasser to licensee or from licensee to invitee.

The lowest in this legal scale is the trespasser, defined as "a person who enters upon land without a privilege to do so".[5] The owner owes no duty to the trespasser to use reasonable care to keep his lands safe for him.

There is an important exception to this rule. If the the trespasser is a child, the degree of obilgation increases. Because of the immaturity of the child, personal judgments on the degree of risk cannot be made. The "attractive nuisance" doctrine grew out of this theory. For instance, if a mine shaft or well is left uncapped and a child traspasser is injured, the owner may be held liable for a breach of duty owed to the child.

The lowest category of persons entitled to use land is the licensee, which is defined as a person who has been given permission to use land with no benefit of the use going to the owner. In most cases, hikers are given the status of licensee. The hiker comes for his own purpose rather than for any purpose of the owner. If he came without a license he would be a

---

[4]*Ibid.*, p. 22.
[5]*Ibid.*, p. 23.

trespasser. The landowner, by giving permission, does *not* extend any assurances that the premises are safe for the purpose for which premission is granted.[6] The duty owed by an owner to a licensee is a negative one. The owner must refrain from malicious and willful failure to warn of or guard against an unseen hazard he knows about. He owes no duty to inspect the premises for safety, nor does he have to warn of hazards that should be obvious to the licensee.

Persons who enter premises for business in which the owner is concerned are given the status of invitees. The historical test of invitee status is whether the owner receives benefit, financial or otherwise, from the person using his land. If a benefit flows to the owner, as would be the case with an entrance fee, then the user would be an invitee. The duty or legal obligation of the owner to an invitee is much greater than the duty owed a licensee. This duty owed is an affirmative one. Not only must the owner protect the invitee from hazards he knows about, he must also protect him against hazards that he, with reasonable care, might discover in insepcting his land.

Financial benefits or benefits in kind are the historical test of invitee status. A newer, more nebulous test, called the invitation test, considers the fact that public trails, open for the purpose of public use, invite use and therefore initiate an invitee status on the user. Opening land to the public implies that it has been prepared for their reception.[7] This theory is being upheld in more and more recent court cases.

The liability of landowners then, in cases other than malicious or willful failure to warn, is a function of the status of use applied to the person using the land.

---

[6]*Ibid.*, p. 23.
[7]*Ibid.*, p. 24.

It seems clear that the hiker is a licensee and as such accepts the risks of his activities as his own. However, to date there has not been enough litigation to supply the precedential standards upon which the distinction between licensee and invitee can be finally and clearly made for all situations. It seems likely that the courts will enforce greater responsilibity on owners in the future because of a generally increasing concern for safety, evident in the consumer movement and in other developing attitudes in our society.

State Laws

Thirty-eight out of forty-seven states in the United States that responded to a survey conducted by the Trails Advisory Committee of Rhode Island[8] have laws whose purpose is to limit the liability of owners who open their land to passive recreational use such as hiking. These laws help to ensure that the duty of owners is the duty owed to a licensee. Lack of court cases, however, has precluded a viable test of these laws. It can be presumed, though, that such laws help to keep the legal obligation of owners at an acceptable level, and that therefore they can be used to inform owners of the limits of the legal risks they will probably incur with public trail use.

These laws help keep liability insurance premiums at a fairly low cost, which consequently makes feasible the purchase of insurance to add protection to landowners who open their lands to recreational use.

Indemnification of landowners by the trail clubs responsible can be tried. However, this should only be done on a case-by-case basis, and then only after a qualified legal opinion has been obtained.

---

[8]Rhode Island State Trail Advisory Committee, *Report of the Trail Advisory Committee*, State of Rhode Island and Bureau of Outdoor Recreation, November, 1974, p. 13.

Insurance[9]

The purpose of insurance is to spread risk over a population large enough so that no insured party would suffer unacceptable losses in the event of a mishap. Insurance is available to private landowners concerned with the liability they may incur by opening land to hiking.

In seeking proper insurance, a local agent is usually in the best position to know a landowner's needs. It is important that this agent understand the nature of the recreational program as well as the volume of recreational use and potential hazards. State laws limiting landowner liability should be brought to the attention of the agent.

Because the insurance market for private recreation facilities is relatively new, it behooves the trail sponsor or owner to seek rates from several companies before making a final choice. Liability insurance covers losses up to policy limits suffered by the owner as a result of a successful lawsuit by an injured hiker. The policy may cover expenses for medical treatment and rescue at the scene of the mishap. It may also cover investigation, defense and settlement costs.

There are two basic types of liability insurance policies available to managers of recreation facilities on private land: the Owner, Landlord, and Tenant Policy (OL&T) and the Comprehensive General Liability Policy.

The OL&T policy is the basic way for covering legal liability to the public. Campgrounds and parking areas may be covered under this type of policy.

---

[9]Bureau of Outdoor Recreation, *Liability and Insurance Protection for Private Recreation Enterprises.*

In the past, many insurance companies have recommended coverage limits of $25,000 per person, $50,000 per accident, and $10,000 in property damages (25/50/10), but because of the increasing amount of court awards and liability claim settlements higher limits should be considered.

The Comprehensive General Liability Policy offers extensive coverage unless specific risks are excluded. Its major advantage for trail use is that it covers almost all hazards.

Overuse, Vandalism, Parking and Other Management Problems

If the owner's reservations regarding future use and liability are quelled, concerns over the actual management of the proposed trail may become the greatest cause for reticence in an owner's support. All of the problems that can develop on public trails can develop on trails in the private sector. These problems range from physical deterioration of soils through erosion to the social problems of overcrowding, vandalism, parking congestion and littering. These problems and their attendant solutions are described in other portions of this book; therefore there is no need to describe them here. A responsible trail organization will make the point to owners that problems have solutions and that these problems will be controlled using proven management techniques.

The basic point, then, is to impart knowledge to the owner and inspire trust in him for the maintenance organization that will be responsible for the trail. It is presumed that the sponsoring organization will have made judgments on its own capabilities to meet this responsibility. This is imperative before winning landowner support for, if management tasks exceed capabilities and problems develop then the owner's trust in the organization will be diminished.

A safe procedure for new trails is to initially limit information on the trail's availability. Management problems are almost directly proportional to the volume of use a trail receives. If the information on a trail is limited, then so is use. Gradually increasing trail information and its subsequent use can give the trail manager the staggered start he needs to increase his management profile with increasing use. In this way problems can be solved at an early stage and not after they become full-blown irritants to the owner. The capability of the maintaining organization will obviously not be as heavily tasked on a trail with low or moderate public use.

Protection of Trails on Private Land

The development and utilization of land protection devices for trail corridors is still a technique that is in the infant stage of development. It is a vast subject that at some stage usually requires legal counsel, considerable expense and time-consuming negotiations. This book can contain only a cursory review of some of the available mechanisms and their benefits and drawbacks when applied to trails.

"A primary concern in initiating an effort to protect a trail is that all persons involved have complete and uniform understanding of the project involved, methods of accomplishing it, and how it is to function and be administered."[10] If policies and modes of implementation are not clearly understood and collectively acknowledged, then negotiations for agreements will not occur.

Skill and enthusiasm on the part of the person carrying out the negotiations with owners is a critical element

---

[10]Platt, Rutherford, *National Symposium on Trails*, Washington, DC, June 2-6, 1971, p. 94.

of success. Likewise, a good public relations profile in the proposed trail region can pave the way to the owner's door. In public relations it is again imperative to stress that the policies underlying implementation of the project be clearly understood. Conflicting information will sow seeds of distrust and reticence in landowners.

It is also imperative that the negotiator be thoroughly familiar with the characteristics of the land on which the trail is proposed. Before approaching an owner, the negotiator should have information on the owner's perspectives and views on trail use. This will greatly facilitate the development of a successful approach to him. It will also help to develop a protective device that best suits his individual needs.

The largest, most sympathetic and most influential owners should be approached first. Owners who seem less supportive can be approached after endorsement from their neighbors is assured.

Although individual adaptions of the trail arrangement for each owner can be made, every owner should have the feeling of being treated equally. If special accommodations are made for one, then dissatisfaction may reign among neighboring owners.

A low-key, soft sell approach reduces the likelihood that an owner will feel threatened. This is especially important in these modern times when the demands on the private sector are growing. Owners feel defensive about ownership; the proper approach is essential to overcoming this defensiveness.

A firmness, however, is also called for. Legal agreements that do not bind the owner to conditions perpetuating a high-quality environment for the trail fail to supply the protection that trails desperately need if they are to fulfill their future role.

In establishing a trail right-of-way there are five legal arrangements that can be made with landowners.[11] These range in legal effect from outright acquisition in fee simple to an informal oral agreement with an owner. Because a legal contract requires a writing, the oral agreement is not legally enforceable and therefore is clearly not appropriate in a trail project except at the initial stages of planning and installation. A complete transfer of ownership may simply not be financially feasible, nor is it necessary except perhaps where permanent facilities such as parking lots and campsites are provided.

Between the two extremes of oral agreement and ownership in fee, there are three limited legal interests that can be placed on trail corridor land. In order according to the extent of the interest, these are the easement, the lease and the license. These non-possessory interests in land offer much flexibility and are excellent techniques for realizing private wishes with respect to the land. Each of these arrangements requires a careful consideration of their respective characteristics.

The easement is the strongest of the non-possessory interests in land. The extent of the interest conveyed needs to be explicitly outlined in the Deed of Conveyance, which is recorded in public records of title. It may be limited to a specific duration or may be granted in perpetuity. Nevertheless, it is binding upon all future owners. With the exception of reverter clauses specifying the termination of interest upon the occurrence of certain events, it is not revocable.

The lease involves an interest in land upon the payment of an agreed-upon fee. It has the advantage to the

---

[11]Crowthers, Leah, in an unpublished work on the Monadnock-Sunapee Greenway Project, sponsored by the Society for the Protection of New Hampshire Forests, Concord, NH, 1974.

landowner of being a terminable arrangement upon the expiration of a certain period of time, but the power of termination is limited to the terms of the written arrangement.

The third and most limited non-possessory interest in land is the license, which is revocable at the will of either party to the agreement. This is the simplest legal device and the least formidable to the owner, who can rest assured that there is no threat of litigation should he decide that the arrangement is no longer in his best interest. The non-binding character of the license makes it fairly easy to consummate with owners; however, it has obvious limitations to the trail interests it protects.

For Further Information

For readers interested in pursuing this subject farther, there are several organizations that specialize in the protection of natural areas. They can be contacted for further information. One such organization is The Nature Conservancy, 294 Washington St., Rm. 850, Boston, MA 02108.

On the state level there are usually organizations that specialize in this kind of conservation work. Among these in New England are:

Society for the Protection of New Hampshire Forests, 5 S. State St., Concord, NH 03301

Maine Coast Heritage Trust, Bar Harbor, ME 04609

Massachusetts Forest & Parks Association, 3 Joy St., Boston, MA 02108

Conservation Law Foundation, 3 Joy Street, Boston, MA 02108

Connecticut Forest & Parks Association, 1010 Main St., PO Box 389, East Hartford, CT 06108

INDEX

Italicized numbers indicate illustrations.